Angle Antics

 Mary Hickey

DEDICATION

To my brother, Richard Daly

Angle Antics©
©1991 by Mary Hickey
That Patchwork Place, Inc.
P.O. Box 118, Bothell, WA 98041-0118

Printed in the British Crown Colony of Hong Kong
98 97 96 95 94 93 92 91 6 5 4 3 2 1

Library of Congress Cataloging-in-Publication Data

Hickey, Mary.
    Angle antics / Mary Hickey; [photography, Brent Kane; illustration and graphics, Stephanie Benson].
        p.   cm.
      "B119"—Cover.
      ISBN 0-943574-76-5
      1. Quilting. 2. Quilting—Patterns. I. Title.
TT835.H448   1991
746.9'7—DC20 90-24773
      CIP

ACKNOWLEDGMENTS

Special thanks are extended to:

    Judy Pollard, for her Wheat Flowers design and quilt;
    Liz Thoman, for her Drumbeat design and quilt;
    Lyn Boland, for her thoughtful suggestions to modify the bias rectangle methods and for the use of her quilts;
    Art Boland, for his mathmatical solutions to several problems;
    Judy Sogn, Nancy Mahoney, Sue Anderson, Suzanne Nelson, Nancy Ewell, Ann Feldman, Joel Patz, Becky Hanson, Susan Stone, Gayle Ducey, and Virginia Lauth, for the use of their quilts;
    Amanda Miller, Dena Yoder, Amanda Yoder, Mary Wengard, Abbie Miller, Freda Smith, and Virginia Lauth, for their fine hand quilting;
    Barbara Wilson, for the generous gift of her time to check numbers;
    Eileen and Steve McAuliffe, for the use of their house; Joan Maricich, for the use of her handmade baskets;
    Phil Hickey, for his endless patience and persistent encouragement.

CREDITS

Photography . . . . Brent Kane
Illustration and Graphics . . . . Stephanie Benson
Text and Cover Design . . . . Judy Petry
Editor . . . . Liz McGehee

Contents

Preface

Among the myriads of quilt designs available, some of the most beautiful are those that include rectangles made up of two long, thin triangles. When these slender triangles are part of a quilt design, wonderful elements emerge: undulating curves and graceful circles, jagged spikes and dynamic zigzags, fragile flowers and sparkling stars. However, if you have ever pieced these long, thin triangles, you know what a nuisance the narrow points can be. The two pieces refuse to line up, and the points insist on creeping into the seam allowance.

In *Little By Little*, I included a pattern for a tiny crocus. The petals of the crocus were cut with a rectangular template placed on bias strips to create tiny, narrow triangles. The response to this method of piecing a difficult shape was favorable, but I was dismayed that the grain lines were "off." Over the next few months, these grain lines haunted me.

Last year, Nancy J. Martin, owner of That Patchwork Place and an accomplished quiltmaker, asked if I would devise a tool for cutting bias rectangles, rectangles made up of two long, thin triangles. I agreed, and the tool that resulted is a bias rectangle ruler, the BiRangle™.

Devising an easy method of cutting strips that would ensure that those ghastly grain lines would be straight took a little longer. After some experimentation, I began teaching an acceptable method.

While teaching these techniques, I received constant feedback from my students. Their feedback enabled me to refine and improve the directions for various quilt plans, so that we now have an efficient way to cut these strips and a quick, accurate method for making bias rectangles.

I hope you will share my fascination and enthusiasm with the extraordinary design potential of this wonderful shape and that you will use the techniques in *Angle Antics* to create your own beautiful quilt.

Introduction

Angle Antics explores the design potential of a rectangle constructed of two contrasting triangles. It also provides you with a technique for constructing this rectangle quickly and accurately. I call this shape a bias rectangle. As a design element, the bias rectangle is quite simple. However, by rotating the direction of the triangles, you can create undulating motions and complex rhythms over the surface of the quilt.

The first part of the book provides complete instructions for an easy, efficient method of constructing the bias rectangle. In addition, there are directions for making bias squares and tips for accurate cutting and precise piecing. For your inspiration, there are diagrams of blocks that incorporate the bias rectangle, some traditional and some original. Twelve quilt plans follow and give detailed instructions for making quilts that use the bias rectangle in a variety of design contexts. Take some time to study the color pictures in the quilt plans and in the Gallery of Quilts. Notice how the quilt artists varied their fabric choices to create diversity, yet order. If you need a refresher on appliqué or finishing techniques, check the Glossary of Techniques on pages 75–78. Templates are provided on pages 79–87 if you prefer a more traditional approach or if you want to check the accuracy of your rotary cutting.

Wheat Flowers (page 62) lends its elegance to this buffet.

A lively Windsor Garden (page 66) brightens this sun-room.

This Meadowlark (page 72) becomes a stunning bed cover and the focal point of the room. The child's rocker holds a folded Double Dutch Chain (page 32).

The soft blues in this Rain Barrel pattern (page 54) are reminiscent of a spring shower.

A Double Dutch Chain (page 32) in traditional reds and greens hangs above the fireplace, while a folded Pondering the Goose warms the hearth (page 44).

Fabrics

I belong to the school of thought that feels you should have a comprehensive fabric collection or library. Quiltmakers seem to share a passion for fabric. Color and visual texture are only part of the motivation for this love. Fabric is tactile, flexible, and forgiving in its manageability. Even its very softness makes it desirable. This ardor for fabric is one of the key bonds that unite quiltmakers from all parts of the world.

It is rarely possible to make a whole quilt just from your fabric collection, but it also may be difficult to make a quilt just from the fabrics available at any one time in the quilt shop. In the past ten years, many quiltmakers have taught themselves the equivalent of a college program in color theory. I think it is important to value yourself as an artist, creating heirlooms for your family, friends, and culture. So, give yourself enough respect to purchase fine cottons and plenty of them to make your quilts. If this makes you feel guilty, think about the money some enthusiasts spend on computer software, or fishing gear, or football tickets. And remember, there are no calories in fabric.

You can see why I have great difficulty in establishing yardage requirements for a quilt plan. (If the quilt takes three yards of background fabric, then I purchase five or six yards so I will have some left to put in my collection.) I also know from teaching classes the problems created by purchasing too little fabric. There is no flexibility to make the quilt bigger, to make a mistake, or to change your mind. So, the fabric requirements given in this book are generous. They are based on yardage that is 42" wide after prewashing. If your fabric is wider than 42", you will have a little left over at the end of your strips. If your fabric is narrower than 42", you may need to cut an extra strip.

The quilts in this book follow a color recipe. The quiltmaker selected a color for a specific unit in the quilt and used it every time that unit appeared. However, the fabrics were varied within that color family. This technique expands the possibilities for adding shading and visual character to the quilt while allowing the quiltmaker to use speed-piecing methods. Each quilt plan in this book has yardage requirements. When working with the bias rectangle, I find it easiest to work with ⅓-yard pieces of fabric. This is a convenient size to handle and enables you to cut about seventy bias rectangles. If a quilt plan calls for more than one ⅓ yard of a bias-rectangle fabric (usually the main fabric), you can switch to another fabric in the same color family with each ⅓ yard you use. Therefore, if the quilt plan calls for 1⅔ yards of fabric to be used in a bias-rectangle unit, you can use up to five different ⅓-yard pieces of similar fabric or 1⅔ yards of any one fabric.

If you have difficulty establishing a color recipe, try selecting one fabric that will inspire you. Often, this one fabric will provide the key to the rest of the colors in the quilt. Look for fabrics in colors related to your main fabric and for colors that will contrast with it. Vary the size and texture of the prints you select. Mix some larger prints with the smaller ones and some linear or geometric ones with flowery ones.

Once you have chosen a group of fabrics, establish a position for each color in the block. Place that color in the same position in each block but feel free to use different fabrics and prints in that position. Be brave and vary the scale of your prints. Use a variety of shades of each color and do not hesitate to do the unexpected.

The ideal fabrics for quilts are lightweight, closely woven 100% cottons. Cotton provides quiltmakers with the ease necessary for smooth, nonpuckered piecing. Prewash all fabrics in warm water. Rinse them until the water is perfectly clear. Dry the fabrics in the dryer and press them before cutting.

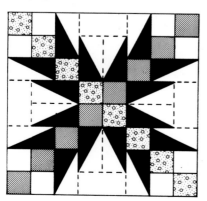

Tools

ROTARY CUTTER AND MAT

A large rotary cutter will enable you to accurately cut strips and pieces. The cutter is placed flush against the ruler to avoid the distortions caused by pencil lines. A sharp rotary blade will cut easily through six or eight layers of fabric. Many cutting mats are available with a 1" grid and a bias or 45° line, which will further aid you in precise cutting.

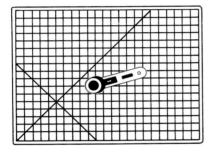

BIRANGLE™

All the quilt plans in this book are based on the use of a bias rectangle. A bias rectangle ruler, or BiRangle™, is the most useful tool for making this unit. It is a 4" x 7½" rectangle made of transparent acrylic and marked with ¼" lines. It also has a diagonal line that will enable you to rapidly cut rectangles made up of contrasting long, thin triangles. The BiRangle is available from That Patchwork Place and is also provided in template form on page 85.

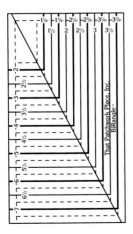

BIAS SQUARE®

A Bias Square® is also very helpful for many of the quilt plans. This tool enables you to cut squares made up of two triangles with great accuracy.

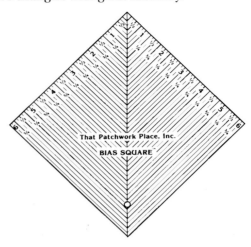

CUTTING GUIDE

A 24" long ruler or cutting guide will enable you to cut the many strips of fabric called for in the quilt plans. A 3½" x 24" ruler is the most convenient size.

SEWING MACHINE

Any machine in good working order can be used to sew quilts, but one with a straight-stitch throat plate will help avoid the problem of your machine chewing the edges of the fabrics. Check the tension on your machine and, if necessary, adjust it so that it will sew a smooth, even seam. Replace the needle with a new one.

Supplies

MARKING TOOLS

Light dashed lines drawn with a sharp pencil are traditionally used to mark quilting lines on quilt tops. A variety of marking tools are available. If you prefer to use a water-soluble pen, test for removability on a scrap before marking the quilt. Chalk dispensers and white pencils are available for marking dark fabrics.

THREAD

Thread for machine piecing may be a light, neutral color, such as beige or gray, for lighter fabrics and a dark neutral for darker fabrics.

Appliqué pieces should be sewn on with thread that matches the color of the appliqué shape, not the background color. For example, a green leaf is stitched on with green thread.

Thread for hand quilting is available in a range of colors. It is thicker than ordinary thread and coated so it does not tangle as readily.

NEEDLES

A supply of sewing machine needles the proper size for your fabric makes it easier for you to piece your blocks precisely. A supply of #10 or #11 Sharp needles is a great asset for hand appliqué. For hand quilting, #9, #10, or #12 Betweens work well.

Accurate Cutting

The cutting measurements given in this book are for rotary cutting and include the ¼" seam allowance. If you prefer to cut with a scissors or want to check the accuracy of your rotary cutting, templates are provided on pages 79–87. Do not add seam allowances to either the rotary cutting instructions or to the templates.

Grain Lines

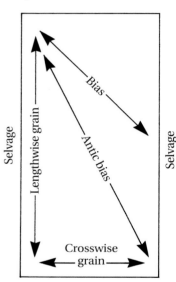

When thread is woven together to form fabric, the lengthwise threads run parallel to the selvage. These threads form the lengthwise grain and are the most stable. The crosswise grain is formed by threads that are perpendicular to the selvage. These threads will have some give or ease. Speed piecing or strip piecing takes advantage of this ease. All other grains are considered bias. A true bias is a line that runs at a 45° angle to the lengthwise and crosswise threads of the fabric.

Angle Antics works with strips cut on the crosswise grain, strips cut on the true bias angle, and strips cut on the not-so-true bias or "antic bias." Start with strips cut on the crosswise grain.

Straight-Cut Strips

All strips include the ¼" seam allowance. If accurate ¼" seams are sewn by machine, there is no need to mark stitching lines on the fabric. To cut squares and rectangles, you will first need to cut straight strips of fabric.

1. Take some time to make sure that your fabric is folded smoothly and that the two selvage edges are perfectly parallel.

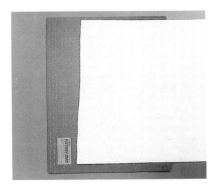

2. Position your folded fabric on your mat. Place your cutting guide on the left and your fabric on the right. (If you are left-handed, reverse these techniques.) Align the fold with one of the grid lines on your mat. (If you do not have grid lines on your mat, align the fold with the edge of the board.) Use the rotary cutter to trim the end of the fabric so that it is exactly perpendicular to the fold.

3. Slide the ruler to the right and measure the width of the strip. Each quilt plan will tell you how wide to cut the strips and how many to cut. Position the proper measurement line on the cut edge of the fabric and cut the required number of strips.

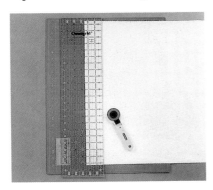

Squares

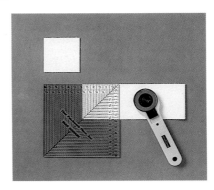

1. Cut the fabric into strips the width specified in the quilt plan.
2. Use a ruler to cut the strips into squares.

Rectangles

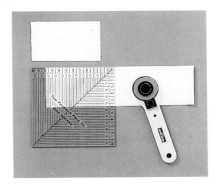

1. Cut the fabric into strips the width specified in the quilt plan.
2. Use a ruler to cut the strips into rectangles of the specified length.

Triangles

A few of the quilt plans call for triangles that are not sewn as squares. It is often efficient to cut these first as squares and then to cut the squares in half on the diagonal or in quarters on the diagonal.

1. Cut a square the size specified in the quilt plan.

2. Cut the square in half on the diagonal. You will have two triangles with the straight grain on the short sides and the bias on the long side.

3. In some quilt plans, you will be asked to cut a square in half on the diagonal and then in half again on the diagonal. You will have four triangles with the straight grain on the long side of the triangles and the bias on the short sides.

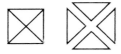

Bias Strip Piecing

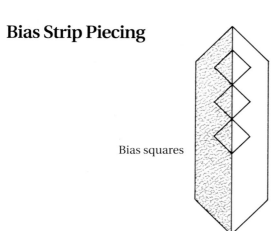

Bias squares

A variety of quilt designs includes squares made from triangles of two contrasting colors. Among the methods devised to enable quiltmakers to quickly piece these triangles, bias strip piecing is by far the most accurate. The short sides of the triangles are on the straight grain, and the long sides are on the bias grain. When the long bias sides are sewn together, the two triangles form a square. These squares are called bias squares.

This technique calls for the quiltmaker to cut bias strips of contrasting fabric, seam the strips together, place the diagonal of a square template on the seam line, then cut the square. Since the sewing and pressing are done before the square is cut, there is little possibility of distorting the square.

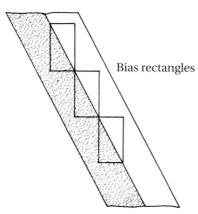

Bias rectangles

Bias Rectangles

Let's take this idea one step further. If the strips are cut on a 64° angle rather than the true bias angle, it is possible to place a rectangular template on the seam line and cut a rectangle made up of two long, thin triangles. Now we have a fast and easy way to piece a unit that has traditionally been rather difficult to sew. If you do not have a bias rectangle ruler, or BiRangle™, you can use the bias rectangle templates provided on page 85.

1. Cut 12" by 42" pieces of your background fabric (fabric A) and your triangle fabric (fabric B). The instructions for each quilt will tell you how many ⅓-yard pieces of each color to cut. To obtain a scrappy look for your quilt, you can change triangle fabrics each time you cut another ⅓ yard.
2. Lay one piece of fabric A on the table face down. Place fabric B on top face down. In other words, layer the two fabrics right side to wrong side.
3. Keep the fabrics layered and fold them in half selvage to selvage. (That's the way they are folded on the bolt.)

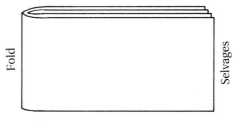

Fold

Selvages

Place fold on left

4. Place the folded fabrics on your cutting board with the fold on the left.
5. If you are making a quilt that requires more than ⅓ yard of each fabric, you can layer and cut up to four folded pieces of fabric at once. Lay another piece of fabric A face down on top of the folded fabrics. Next, lay a piece of fabric B face down on top of it. Keep the fabrics layered and fold them in half. You should have two sets of folded fabric, one on top of the other. (When cutting multiple layers, it is helpful to have a sharp blade in your rotary cutter.) If your quilt plan calls for three, four, or five ⅓-yard pieces, you will need to repeat this procedure because eight layers of fabric are as much as most rotary cutters can manage.

6. Use the rotary cutter to trim a straight edge off the top, perpendicular to the selvage.

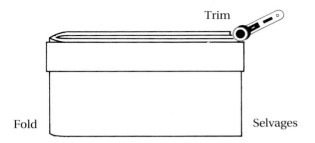

Trim

Fold   Selvages

7. Place the BiRangle™ on the upper edge of the fabrics so that the diagonal line points from the upper edge of the fabrics to the lower right-hand corner of the fabrics. (The angle line of the ruler will be about 5 ¾" from the selvage edge.)

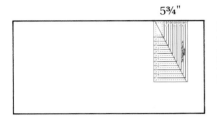

5¾"

Place BiRangle™ with diagonal line pointing toward lower right-hand corner

8. Lay your cutting guide on the diagonal line of the BiRangle. The placement of the ruler creates an angle across the fabric.

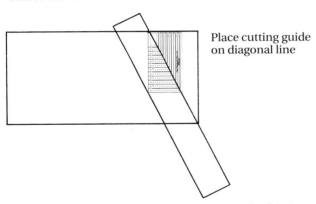

Place cutting guide on diagonal line

9. Slide the BiRangle out of the way and cut the fabric on the right side of the ruler from the bottom to the top.

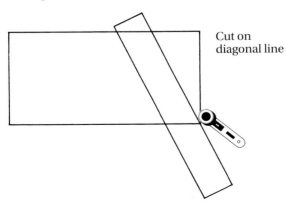

Cut on diagonal line

10. Cut six sets of strips parallel to this first angled cut. A chart on page 17 provides the widths of the strips to cut for the size rectangle needed. For all of the quilts in this book, except Regatta, cut the strips 2½" wide. (See pages 41–42 for Regatta directions.) DO NOT MOVE THE STRIPS YET.

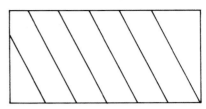

Cut strips parallel to first cut

11. Without disturbing the strips, remove the large left-over end pieces and set them aside. (These leftover pieces can be stitched together along the angled side to form longer lengths of fabric for binding. You also can use them for other parts of the quilt—or save them for a scrap quilt.)

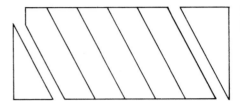

Remove leftover pieces

Because the fabrics were folded, some strips will have right sides facing up and some will have right sides facing down. Place the ones facing up, on the right and the ones facing down, on the left. Depending on which direction the strips are facing, some will be made into rectangles with the fabric B triangles on the right and some with the fabric B triangles on the left. This is why the strips are sorted into two sets. Try to avoid moving them around because it is difficult to tell the right from the wrong side if you are working with fabrics that do not have a printed design. If the strips are placed in the wrong set, the grain lines will be going the wrong direction.

12. Take twelve of the strips on the right and, without turning any over, arrange them into a unit of strips, alternating the fabrics. With right sides together, sew strips, offsetting the tops of strips ¼" so that they form an even angled line across the top of the unit.

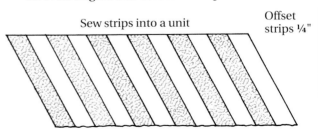

Sew strips into a unit   Offset strips ¼"

13. Press the seams open. Don't worry if one end of the unit is a bit ragged.

14. Sew and press the left set into a unit. The strips will slope in the opposite direction from the first set.

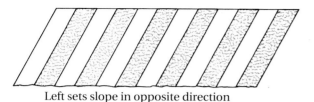

Left sets slope in opposite direction

15. Continue to sew units from twelve strips of fabric, as outlined above, keeping the left sets separated from the right sets.

16. Position your BiRangle on top of one of these units with the diagonal line on the center seam line. Slide the BiRangle up, near the top of the unit. If the edge of the BiRangle is parallel to the top of the unit, use the upper edge of the BiRangle to guide you as you trim off the top edge of the unit. If the edge of the BiRangle is not parallel to the top of the unit, either turn the BiRangle over or turn the fabric unit over. Once the BiRangle is in place, trim an even angled edge across the top of the unit.

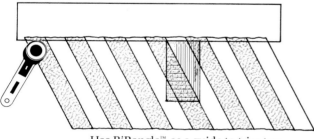

Use BiRangle™ as a guide to trim top

17. Cut segments parallel to the trimmed edge. For all of the quilts in this book, except Regatta, cut the segments 3½" wide. (Complete directions for making Regatta are on pages 41–42.) *Before you cut each segment, check and correct the angle of the upper edge by repeating step 16.*

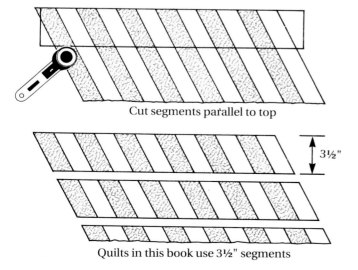

Cut segments parallel to top

3½"

Quilts in this book use 3½" segments

18. Sew three of the segments together end to end to create longer segments. You can sew more than three segments together but you must be careful not to stretch the bias. By sewing the ends together, you avoid wasting the triangle at the end of the segment.

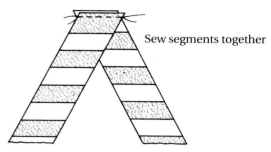

Sew segments together

19. With the diagonal line on the seam line, place the BiRangle on one of the segments. Look at the grain lines on the fabrics. If the grain lines are parallel to the edges of the BiRangle, you are ready to cut. Notice that the diagonal line of the BiRangle lies ⅛" from the corner of the rectangle. This is the correct position. Use the edge of the BiRangle to cut one side of the rectangle.

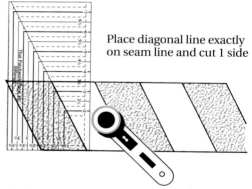

Place diagonal line exactly on seam line and cut 1 side

Turn the fabrics around and measure 2" (2" is the correct width for all the quilt plans in this book except Regatta) and cut the other side of the rectangle.

Turn fabrics and cut other side

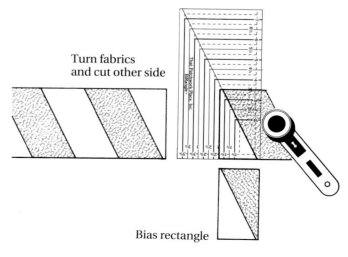

Bias rectangle

It is important to position the diagonal line of the BiRangle exactly on the seam line of the fabrics. Again, make sure the grain lines of the fabrics are parallel to the straight lines of the BiRangle. If they are not, turn the BiRangle over or turn the segment face down. Take an extra second to cut carefully. Accuracy at this point will save time and frustration later when you are assembling the blocks.

From one of the units, you will be cutting rectangles with fabric B on the right, and from the other, you will be cutting rectangles with fabric B on the left. Usually, two pieces (⅓ yard each) will yield seventy bias rectangles. The instructions for each quilt will specify how many bias rectangles of each fabric combination to cut.

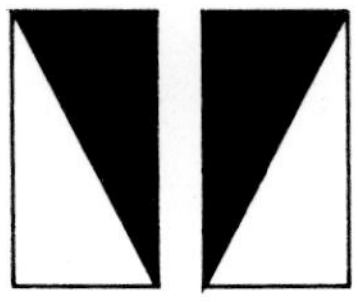

If you find it too tedious to cut all of them at once (I do!), cut about thirty-five of each piece and go on to the next steps. Once you have the strips organized and sewn, you'll find it easy to cut more rectangles.

Width of Diagonal Strips

The width of the diagonal strips that you cut will depend on the size of rectangle you wish to make. Generally, the width of the diagonal strip, the distance across the strip perpendicular to the sides, is 1" larger than the finished width (without the ¼" seam allowances) of your rectangle's short side.

FINISHED RECTANGLE		WIDTH OF DIAGONAL STRIP
Short Side	Long Side	
¾"	1½"	1¾"
1"	2"	2"
1¼"	2½"	2¼"
1½"	3"	2½"
1¾"	3½"	2¾"
2"	4"	3"
2¼"	4½"	3¼"
2½"	5"	3½"
2¾"	5½"	3¾"
3"	6"	4"
3¼"	6½"	4¼"
3½"	7"	4½"

Bias Squares

   Bias squares

Bias strip piecing has already been discussed as the most accurate method for creating bias squares (see page 14). Long bias strips are sewn together in pairs and squares made up of two triangles are cut from the sewn bias strips. This method takes a little longer than speed- or sandwich-pieced triangles but it is so much more accurate that it saves time and frustration later when assembling the blocks.

It is easiest to work with ⅓-yard pieces of fabric. The instructions for each quilt will tell you how many ⅓-yard pieces of each fabric to use and how many bias squares to cut. You can layer several fabrics at once to cut the bias strips. Be sure to place all fabrics right side to wrong side. In other words, layer all fabrics face up.

1. Layer fabric A (background) and fabric B (main) right side to wrong side.
2. Draw a bias line on the top fabric.

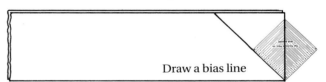

Draw a bias line

3. Cut bias strips parallel to the drawn line. The instructions for each quilt will tell you how many strips to cut and how wide to cut the strips. In general, cut the strips the width of the finished square, plus ¼".

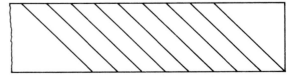

Cut strips parallel to bias line

4. Sew the strips together into units of eight strips each. Alternate the fabrics in each unit and press toward the darker color.

Sew strips into a unit

5. Place the unit on your cutting board.
6. Position the Bias Square® with its diagonal line on the seam line. Slide the Bias Square toward the top of the unit. Using the upper edge of the Bias Square to guide you, place your long cutting guide across the top of the unit. Trim an even edge across the top.

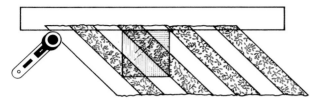

Use Bias Square® as a guide to trim top

7. Cut a segment parallel to the first cut. Each quilt plan will tell you how wide to cut this segment.

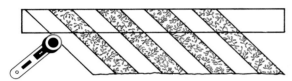

Cut strips parallel to top

8. Use the technique in step 6 to check and correct the angle along the top of the unit before cutting each segment.
9. Cut another segment the width specified in the quilt instructions.
10. Continue cutting segments from the unit; *be sure to check and correct the angle after each cut.*

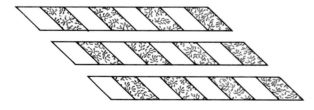

11. Sew three segments together end to end to create one long segment. You can sew more than three segments together, but you must be careful not to stretch the bias. By seaming the segments together, you avoid wasting the triangle on the end of the unit.

12. Lay one of the segments on your cutting mat. Place the Bias Square® with the diagonal line on the seam line and one edge of the Bias Square on the cut edge of the segment. Cut on one side.

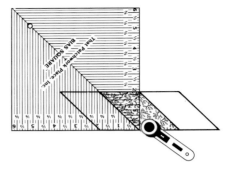

Place diagonal line on seam and cut first side

Rotate the fabrics, reposition the diagonal line, and cut the other side.

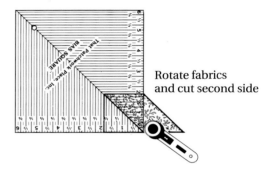

Rotate fabrics and cut second side

(I usually cut the whole strip with the Bias Square pointing in one direction and then rotate the Bias Square and trim the other sides in that direction.)

13. Continue to cut in this manner until you have the specified number of bias squares.

Precise Machine Piecing

When quiltmakers sew a block, they stitch small geometric shapes to each other to form units. These units are joined to make larger units and these, in turn, are sewn together to create the block. When speed piecing, they sew strips of fabric together and cut some of the units from the sewn strips. In both methods, fabrics must be cut precisely and sewn accurately so that the whole quilt will match correctly. Keep the following tips in mind as you sew.

1. **Sewing exact seams.** Sew exact ¼" seams. Check your presser foot to determine if it is ¼" wide. Place a template under the presser foot and position the needle so it pierces exactly through the seam line. The distance from the seam line to the edge of the template is ¼". Lay a piece of masking tape next to the edge of the template to act as a seam guide. Stitch length should be set at ten to twelve stitches per inch.

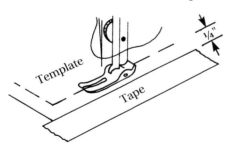

2. **Pressing.** The seams of bias rectangle strips should be pressed open. These open seams will enable you to piece the bias rectangles into the blocks with ease and accuracy. In general, other seams should be pressed toward the darker-colored fabric. In a few instances, you may be asked to press all seams in a specific direction; for instance, when it is desirable to have opposing seams.

3. **Chain stitching.** Whenever possible, chain stitch the pieces you are sewing together. Sew a seam and, without taking the piece out of the machine or cutting the threads, sew the next piece.

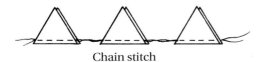

Chain stitch

4. **Easing.** If a piece is shorter than the one it is supposed to match, place both pieces under the presser foot, with the shorter piece on top. Use a large tapestry needle or your seam ripper to hold together the points of matching and sew. The feed dog will help ease in the fullness of the longer piece on the bottom.

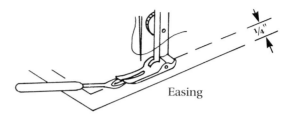

Easing

5. **Matching opposing seams.** Many corners and points can be matched easily by pressing the seams that need to match in opposite directions. The opposing seam allowances will help hold the points of matching in place.

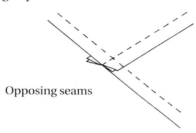

Opposing seams

In some quilt plans, blocks are sewn directly to one another without sashings or set pieces. Matching the points of these blocks can be particularly difficult. One way to overcome this difficulty is to ignore the old quilting maxim of pressing toward the darker color; instead, press seams in opposite directions. For this reason, in certain quilts (Byzantine Star, Rain Barrel, Meadowlark, and Drumbeat), it is a good idea to designate some blocks as A blocks and some blocks as B blocks.

As you stitch the units of the A blocks, press all the seams toward the lighter colors. As you stitch the B blocks, press all seams toward the darker colors. This pressing strategy will create opposing seams between the blocks.

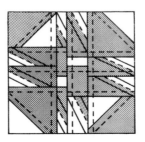

Block A
Press toward
lighter colors

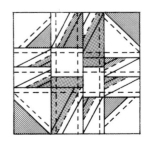

Block B
Press toward
darker colors

6. Aiming for the X. When you sew pairs of triangles to each other, the stitching lines cross each other on the back, creating an X. As you sew triangle units, aim your stitching through the X to obtain crisp points on your triangles.

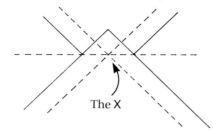

The X

A variety of blocks can be designed using narrow triangles. A few traditional and original ones are illustrated below to help inspire you.

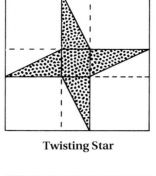

Twisting Star

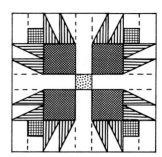

Mother Bear

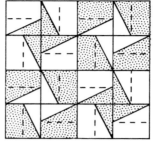

Shooting Star

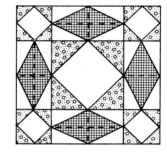

**Rolling Stone
(Storm at Sea variation)**

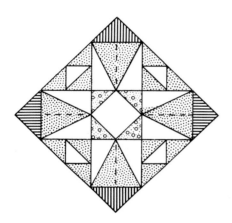

Western Star

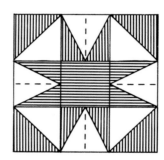

Eight-Pointed Star

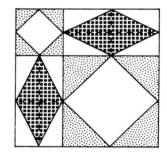

Storm at Sea

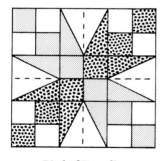

Bird of Paradise

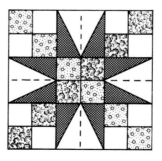

**Sun Ray's Quilt
Darting Minnows**

Fifty-four Forty or Fight

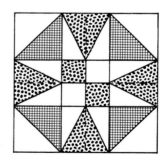

Judy in Arabia

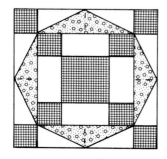

Robin's Nest

Doris's Delight

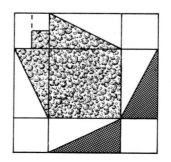

Magnolia Blossom

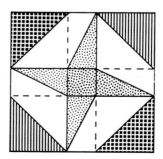

Star Gazing

Gallery of Quilts

Spring Rain (Rain Barrel) *by Mary Hickey, 1990, Seattle, Washington, 52" x 66". A soft wash of blue prints gives this interpretation of the Rain Barrel pattern the transparent effect of a watercolor painting.*

St. Benedict's Star *by Gayle Ducey, 1990, Seattle, Washington, 46" x 46". An exuberant floral border sets the color scheme of this handsome wall hanging.*

Double Dutch Chain *by Nancy Ewell, 1990, Seattle, Washington, 43" x 43". Delicate green chains and soft peach tulips surounded by a printed ribbon border create this cheerful quilt.*

Dementia 401 (Meadowlark) *by Lyn Boland, 1990, Issaquah, Washington, 60" x 64". Hundreds of different fabrics, intricate shading, and masterful piecing radiate light and energy across the surface of this stunning quilt.*

Pondering the Goose *by Susan Stone, 1990, Edmonds, Washington, 88" x 100". Soft, misty pinks, crisp whites, and a lovely black floral create this romantic quilt.*

Byzantine Star *by Sue Anderson, 1990, Seattle, Washington, 62" x 70". A variety of colors progressing from light to dark creates vibrant stars amid a glowing background.*

*Zimbabwe Star (**St. Benedict's Star**) by Joel T. Patz, 1990, Seattle, Washington, 62" x 74". Subtle stripes, artfully arranged and carefully pieced, produce a shimmering movement in this striking quilt.*

*Carpe Diem (**St. Benedict's Star**) by Ann Feldman, 1990, Seattle, Washington, 88" x 104". The whimsical fish fabric sets a light-hearted mood for this striking quilt.*

Windsor Garden by Mary Hickey, 1990, Seattle, Washington, 48" x 48". Warm reds and muted greens enhance the cheerful, spontaneous quality of this pattern.

Wheat Flowers by Virginia Lauth, 1990, Seattle, Washington, 36" x 42". A bold combination of blacks, purples, and turquoise enhances the romantic allure of this exotic bouquet.

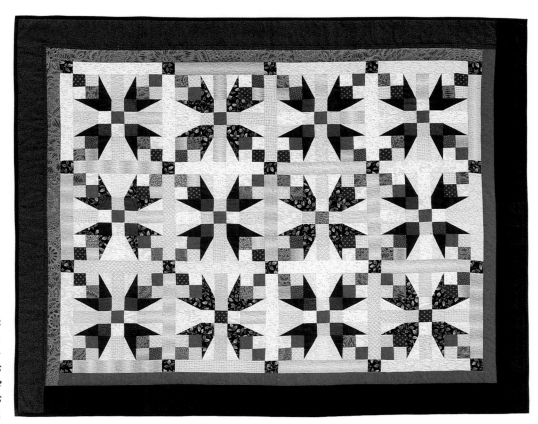

Noel (Double Dutch Chain) by Mary Hickey, 1990, Seattle, Washington, 50" x 60". Barn reds and forest greens provide a warm, cozy Christmas focal point.

Double Dutch Chain by Gayle Ducey, 1990, Seattle, Washington, 46" x 46". Calm blues, carefully pieced, create this clean, elegant interpretation of the Double Dutch Chain.

Stars All Around by Becky Hanson, 1990, Everett, Washington, 40" x 40". Simple blocks in two different color combinations create a complex pattern.

Quilt Plans

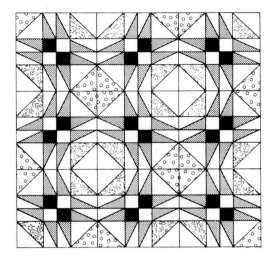

This section contains twelve complete plans for quilts that incorporate the bias-rectangle unit as a design element. Each plan includes quilt dimensions with and without borders, fabric requirements, step-by-step cutting instructions, piecing diagrams, and a color photo of the quilt.

The cutting instructions are written for rotary cutting and include ¼" seam allowances. The letter designations in the block diagram illustrate fabric positions. In all the quilts except Regatta, the cut size of the bias rectangles is 2" x 3½".

Some quiltmakers find Template-Free™ techniques confusing because they are not sure what shape they are cutting or what part of the block they are making. For this reason, a small icon (illustration) is printed next to each instruction to clarify which part of the block you are making as you do your speed piecing.

Master templates are found on pages 80–84. Use the templates if you prefer to cut with a scissors or if you wish to make just one block as a test sample. The templates include ¼" seam allowances. The quilt plans for Wheat Flowers and Windsor Garden include template references for appliqué leaves and the pieced portions of the quilts. However, for some of the large pieces, you'll find instructions for measuring and cutting these pieces without a template. All measurements include the ¼" seam allowance.

Consult the Glossary of Techniques on pages 75–78 for appliqué instructions and directions on quilt finishing methods.

St. Benedict's Star

St. Benedict's Star *by Mary Hickey, 1990, Seattle, Washington, 84½" x 109½". The small twisting star in the center of each block creates interest and energy in this striking pattern.*

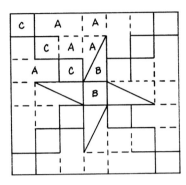

Large Star block

Small Star block

Block size (finished): 10½"
Pieced area of quilt: 61½" x 85½"
Quilt with borders: 84½" x 109½"

Materials: (44"–45" wide fabric)

6 yds. fabric A (background)
2½ yds. fabric B (main)
1½ yds. fabric C (chain)
¾ yd. inner border fabric
3¼ yds. outer border fabric

Optional templates (for scissors cutting): 1, 2, 3, 17

Unit Instructions

Bias Rectangles

2" x 3½"

1. Cut: 4 pieces fabric A, 12" x 42"
   4 pieces fabric B, 12" x 42"
2. Following the instructions on pages 14–17, cut and sew 284 bias rectangles. You need 142 with fabric B on the right and 142 with fabric B on the left.

Strips

Cut: 24 strips fabric A, 2" x 42"
7 strips fabric A, 3½" x 42"
19 strips fabric C, 2" x 42"
These strips will be used to make the remaining units.

Squares

 2" x 2"

Cut 9 fabric A strips, 2" x 42", into 2" squares. You need 212 squares.

Four Patches

1. Sew 8 fabric A strips, 2" x 42", and 8 fabric C strips, 2" x 42", together in pairs.
2. Press toward the darker color.
3. Layer the sewn pairs right sides together with opposite fabrics facing each other.

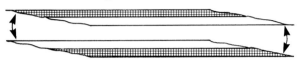

4. Cut across the layered strips at 2" intervals, creating rectangles made up of 2 pairs.

5. Stitch the rectangles together into 72 Four Patches.

Modified Ninepatches

1. Cut 1 fabric A strip and 1 fabric C strip in half.
2. Sew the half strips, 6 fabric A strips, 2" x 42", and 3 fabric C strips, 2" x 42" into 3½ units made up of A-C-A.

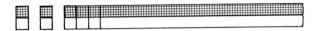 A
C
A

3. Layer these units and cut across them at 2" intervals, creating rectangles. You need 68.

4. Sew 7 units made up of a 2" fabric C strip and a 3½" fabric A strip as illustrated.

 C
A

5. Layer these units and cut across them at 2" intervals, creating rectangles. You need 136.

6. Stitch the rectangles together as illustrated to make the modified Ninepatches.

Assembling the Blocks

1. Assemble 18 large Star blocks as illustrated.

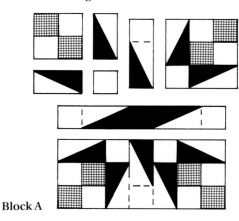

Block A

2. Assemble 17 small Star blocks as illustrated.

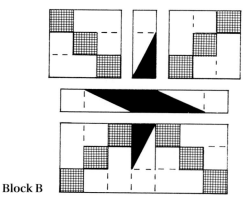

Block B

Sashing

1. Cut: 27 strips fabric A, 2" x 42"
      3 strips fabric C, 2" x 42"
2. Cut the fabric C strips into 2" squares. You need 48 squares.

2" x 2"

3. Cut the fabric A strips into 2" x 11" pieces. You need 82 pieces.

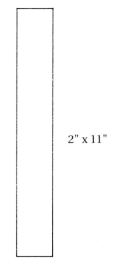

2" x 11"

Assemble the quilt top as illustrated on page 31.

Borders

1. Cut and sew: 2 strips inner border fabric, 2" x 67"
                2 strips inner border fabric, 2" x 92"
2. Cut and sew: 2 strips outer border fabric, 10" x 90"
                2 strips outer border fabric, 10" x 112"
3. Sew the border strips to each other in pairs.
4. Stitch the borders to the quilt top, mitering the corners (see Mitering Corners, pages 76–77). Trim corners as necessary.

Finishing

1. Layer the quilt top with batting and backing.
2. Baste, quilt, and bind.

Double Dutch Chain

January Sunshine (Double Dutch Chain) *by Mary Hickey, 1990, Seattle, Washington, 75" x 86". Two bias rectangles combine with a square to create a tulip shape. Continuing squares form a chain linking the tulips across the surface of the quilt.*

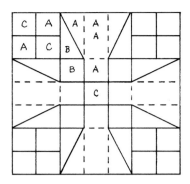

Block size (finished): 10½"
Pieced area of quilt: 61½" x 73½"
Quilt size with borders: 75" x 86"

Materials: (44"–45" wide fabric)

5½ yds. fabric A (background)
3 yds. fabric B (main)
1 yd. fabric C (chain)
½ yd. inner border fabric
1½ yds. outer border fabric

Optional templates (for scissors cutting): 1, 2, 3, 17

Unit Instructions

Bias Rectangles

 2" x 3½"

1. Cut: 4 pieces fabric A, 12" x 42"
   4 pieces fabric B, 12" x 42"
2. Following the instructions on pages 14–17, cut and sew 240 bias rectangles. You need 120 with fabric B on the right and 120 with fabric B on the left.

Strips

Cut: 23 strips fabric A, 2" x 42"
8 strips fabric B, 2" x 42"
8 strips fabric C, 2" x 42"
These strips will be used to make the remaining units.

Rectangles

Cut 10 of the fabric A strips into rectangles, 2" x 3½". You need 120 rectangles.

2" x 3½"

Four Patches

1. Sew 6 of the fabric A strips to 6 of the fabric C strips in pairs. Press toward the C strips.

2. Layer the pairs right sides together with opposite fabrics facing each other.

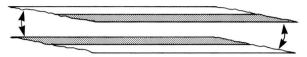

3. Cut across the layered strips at 2" intervals, creating rectangles made up of 2 squares.

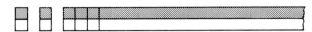

4. Sew the rectangles together in pairs, creating Four Patches. You need 120.

Ninepatches

1. Sew 3 of the fabric A strips and 6 of the fabric B strips into 3 units, each made up of B-A-B.

2. Sew 4 of the fabric A strips and 2 of the fabric C strips into 2 units, each made up of A-C-A.

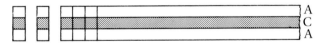

3. Cut across the units of strips at 2" intervals, creating rectangles made up of 3 squares.
4. Stitch the rectangles together as illustrated to make 30 Ninepatches.

Assemble the blocks as illustrated.

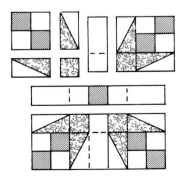
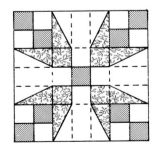

Sashing

1. Cut: 23 strips fabric A, 2" x 42"
   2 strips fabric C, 2" x 42"
2. Cut the fabric C strips into 2" squares. You need 42 of them.

2" x 2"

3. Cut the fabric A strips into 2" x 11" rectangles. You need 71 of them.

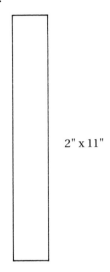
2" x 11"

Assemble the quilt top as illustrated.

Borders

1. Cut and sew: 2 strips inner border fabric, 1¼" x 66"
   2 strips inner border fabric, 1¼" x 80"
2. Cut and sew: 2 strips outer border fabric, 5" x 69"
   2 strips outer border fabric, 5" x 90"
3. Sew the inner border strips to the outer border strips in pairs.
4. Stitch the sewn border strips to the quilt top, mitering the corners (see Mitering Corners, pages 76–77). Trim as necessary.

Finishing

1. Layer the quilt top with batting and backing.
2. Baste, quilt, and bind.

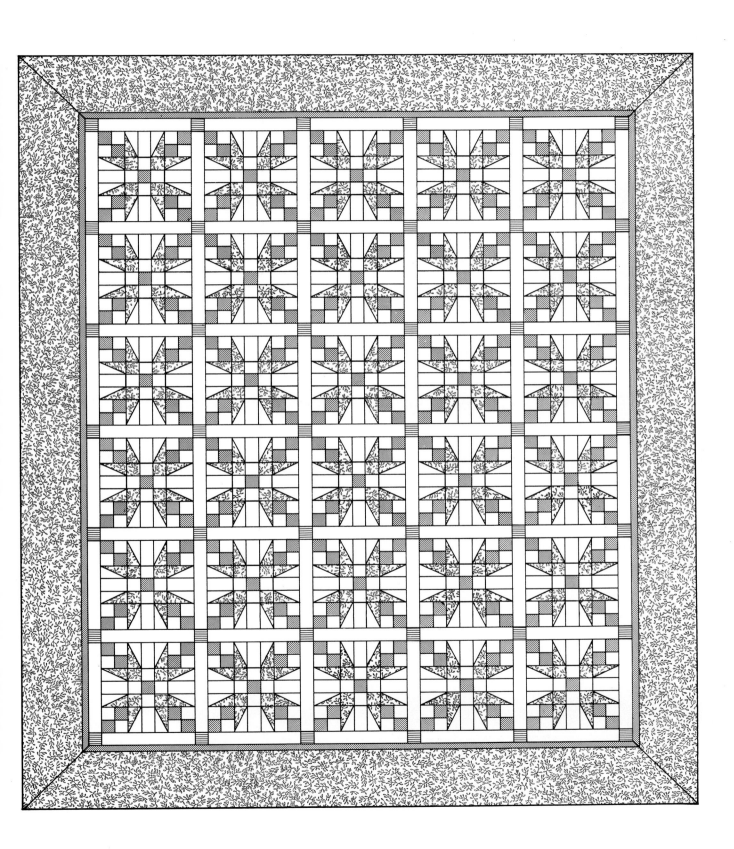

Byzantine Star

Rose Galaxy (Byzantine Star) *by Nancy Mahoney, 1990, Seattle, Washington, 64" x 76½". Simple shapes, artfully combined, create this exceptional quilt. Careful placement of the colors in the Four Patches creates rose chains moving between the stars in one direction and gray chains in the other direction.*

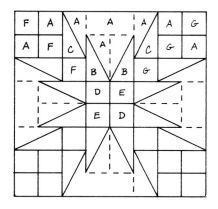

Block size (finished): 12½"
Pieced area of quilt: 50" x 62½"
Quilt with borders: 62" x 74½"

Although this block looks complicated, it is constructed of very simple quilting units: triangle pairs, Four Patches, squares, and rectangles. The pattern lends itself to a scrappy look, but to make any sense out of the design, it is best to designate certain colors for certain parts of the block and to stick to that designation in every block. The fabric print and the intensity of its color can change, but the color itself should remain constant from block to block. Also, you may want to use a color gradation in this block design. That is, try to work from light to dark.

Materials: (44"–45" wide fabric)

4½ yds. fabric A (background)
¾ yd. fabric B (inner bias rectangles)
¾ yd. fabric C (outer bias rectangles)
¼ yd. fabric D (inner Four Patches)
¼ yd. fabric E (inner Four Patches)
⅝ yd. fabric F (outer Four Patches)
⅝ yd. fabric G (outer Four Patches)
½ yd. inner border fabric
1½ yds. outer border fabric

Optional templates (for scissors cutting): 1, 2, 3

Unit Instructions

Bias Rectangles

2" x 3½"

1. Cut: 2 pieces fabric A, 12" x 42"
   2 pieces fabric B, 12" x 42"
2. Following the instructions on pages 14–17, cut and sew 160 bias rectangles. You need 80 with fabric B on the right and 80 with fabric B on the left.

2" x 3½"

3. Cut: 2 pieces fabric A, 12" x 42"
   2 pieces fabric C, 12" x 42"
4. Following the instructions on pages 14–17, cut and sew 160 bias rectangles. You need 80 with fabric C on the right and 80 with fabric C on the left.

Rectangles and Squares

1. Cut 4 strips fabric A, 3½" x 42".
2. Layer the strips and cut across them at 2" intervals to make 2" x 3½" rectangles. You need 80 rectangles.

2" x 3½"

3. Cut 2 strips each of fabrics F and G, 2" x 42".
4. Layer the fabric F and G strips and cut them into 2" squares. You need 80 squares.

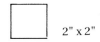

2" x 2"

Inner Four Patches

1. Cut: 2 strips fabric D, 2" x 42"
   2 strips fabric E, 2" x 42"
2. Sew the strips together in pairs and press toward the darker color.
3. Layer the sewn pairs right sides together with opposite fabrics facing each other.

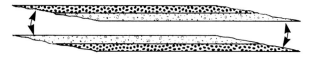

4. Cut across the layered strips at 2" intervals, creating rectangles.

5. Stitch the rectangles together to make 20 Four Patches.

Outer Four Patches

1. Cut: 8 strips fabric A, 2" x 42"
   4 strips fabric F, 2" x 42"
   4 strips fabric G, 2" x 42"
2. Sew the strips together in pairs with a fabric A strip in every pair.
3. Layer the sewn strips in pairs right sides together. Place an A-G pair right sides together with an A-F pair so that fabric G faces fabric A of the other pair. These pairs will then be ready to stitch after they're cut.

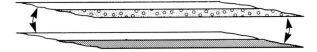

4. Cut across the layered strips at 2" intervals, creating rectangles.

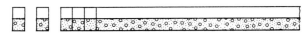

5. Sew the rectangles together to make 80 Four Patches. Notice that the quilt in the photograph has the roses going in one direction and the grays going in the other direction.

Assembling the Blocks

1. The blocks in this quilt are stitched directly to each other without sashing or set blocks. To make it easier to match all points, designate blocks as either A or B and press to obtain opposing seams (see page 19).

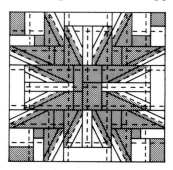 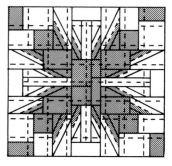

Block A
Press toward lighter colors

Block B
Press toward darker colors

2. Assemble the blocks as illustrated using the Four Patches as previously pressed.

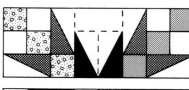

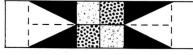

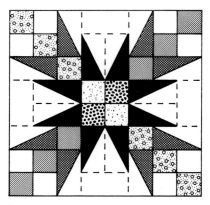

Assembling the Quilt Top

1. Sew the blocks together into rows, alternating A and B blocks.
2. Stitch the rows together to make the quilt top as shown on page 39.

Borders

1. Cut and sew: 2 strips inner border fabric, 2" x 56"
   2 strips inner border fabric, 2" x 68½"
2. Cut and sew: 2 strips outer border fabric, 5" x 62"
   2 strips outer border fabric, 5" x 74½"
3. Sew the borders to the quilt top, mitering the corners (see Mitering Corners, pages 76–77). Trim as necessary.

Finishing

1. Layer the quilt top with backing and batting.
2. Baste, quilt, and bind.

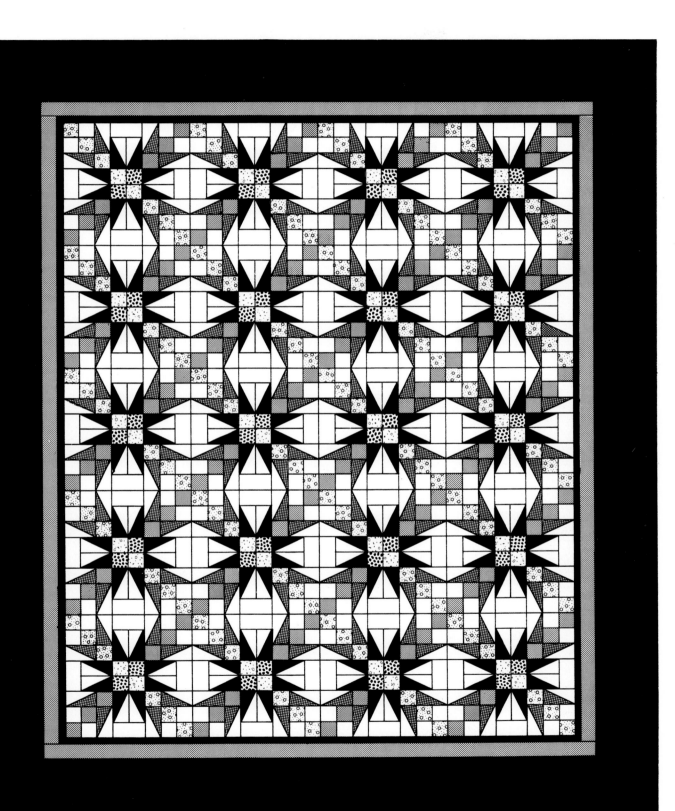

Regatta

Regatta *by Mary Hickey, 1990, Seattle, Washington, 61" x 94½". The batik waves form an effective sashing for these jaunty sailboats bouncing across the quilt.*

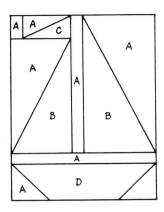

Block size (finished): 6" x 8"
Pieced area of quilt: 38" x 71½"
Quilt with borders: 61" x 94½" (bunk bed or captain's bed size)

Materials: (44"–45" wide fabric)

2½ yds. fabric A (background)
1½ yds. fabric B (sails)
¼ yd. fabric C (flags)
¼ yd. fabric D or scraps totaling ¼ yd. (boat hulls)
¾ yd. horizontal sashing fabric
⅓ yd. inner border fabric
2½ yds. outer border fabric

Optional templates (for scissors cutting):
5, 6, 7, 8, 9, 10, 13

Unit Instructions

SAILS

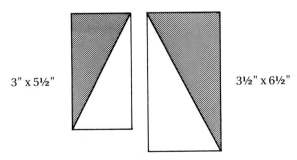

3" x 5½"   3½" x 6½"

1. Cut: 2 pieces fabric A, 14" x 42"
    2 pieces fabric B, 14" x 42"
2. Following the instructions on pages 14–17, cut and sew 48 bias rectangles. Cut the strips 4" wide, then cut the units according to the chart below. Or, mix the units and have some going one direction and some going the other. Regattas are like that.

| Left unit | cut 3" x 5½" | finish 2½" x 5" |
| Right unit | cut 3½" x 6½" | finish 3" x 6" |

FLAGS

          1½" x 2½"

1. Cut: 1 piece fabric A, 9" x 22"
    1 piece fabric C, 9" x 22"
2. Layering the fabrics right side to wrong side and following instructions on pages 14–17, cut and sew 4 strips 2" wide. Cut 24 bias rectangles 1½" x 2½". Do not fold the fabrics when cutting the strips, unless you are having the boats sail in both directions.

HULLS

Whether it is easier to cut and sew the boat hulls from strips or to use templates is a toss-up. For those of you who are philosophically opposed to templates, here is a nifty way to make the boat hulls from strips.

1. Cut 2 strips fabric A, 2" x 42".
2. Cut the strips into 2" squares. You need 50 squares.

          2" x 2"

3. Cut 4 strips fabric D, 2" x 42".
4. Cut the strips into 2" x 6½" rectangles. You need 25 rectangles.

   2" x 6½"

5. Lay a fabric A square on each end of a boat-hull rectangle.
6. Sew the squares to the boat hull by stitching a diagonal line from corner to corner on each square as illustrated.

Stitch diagonally   Boat hull
across squares and trim

SPACER STRIPS

1. Cut 9 strips fabric A, 1" x 42".
2. Cut 8 of these strips into thin rectangles, 1" x 6½". You need 48 rectangles. These pieces go between the sails and between the pairs of sails and the boat hulls.

   1" x 6½"

3. Cut the remaining strip into small rectangles, 1" x 1½". You need 24 rectangles. These pieces go between the tip of the flag and the edge of the block.

          1" x 1½"

Assemble the blocks as illustrated.

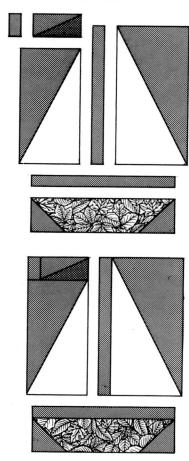

Vertical Sashing

1. Cut 5 rectangles from fabric A, 6½" x 8½". These are used as spacer blocks in rows 1–4 and row 6.
2. Cut 5 strips fabric A, 2½" x 42".
3. Cut the strips into 2½" x 8½" rectangles. You need 20 rectangles for sashing between the boats in rows 1–4 and row 6.
4. An inexperienced sailor has capsized in row 5—a most embarrassing occurrence and always a nuisance, even for the quiltmaker.
   From fabric A, cut: 1 piece, 6½" x 7"
                         3 pieces, 1½" x 8½"
                         1 piece, 2" x 8½"
                         2 pieces, 2½" x 8½"
5. Assemble row 5 as illustrated.

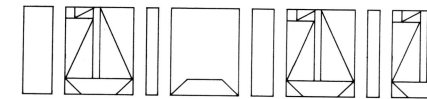

6. Assemble rows 1–4 and row 6 as illustrated on page 43.

Horizontal Sashing

1. Cut 1 sashing strip fabric A, 3½" x 42", to sew on the top of row 1.
2. Cut 5 strips of sashing fabric, 3½" x 42", to sew on the bottoms of rows 1–5.
3. Cut 1 strip of sashing fabric, 6" x 42", to sew on the bottom of row 6.

Assemble the quilt top as illustrated. Trim sashing where necessary.

Borders

1. Cut and sew: 2 strips inner border fabric, 1½" x 45"
                         2 strips inner border fabric, 1½" x 78"
2. Cut and sew: 2 outer border strips, 10" x 65"
                         2 outer border strips, 10" x 98"
3. Stitch borders to each other in pairs.
4. Sew borders to the quilt top, mitering corners (see Mitering Corners, pages 76–77). Trim as necessary.

Finishing

1. Layer the quilt top with batting and backing.
2. Baste, quilt, and bind.

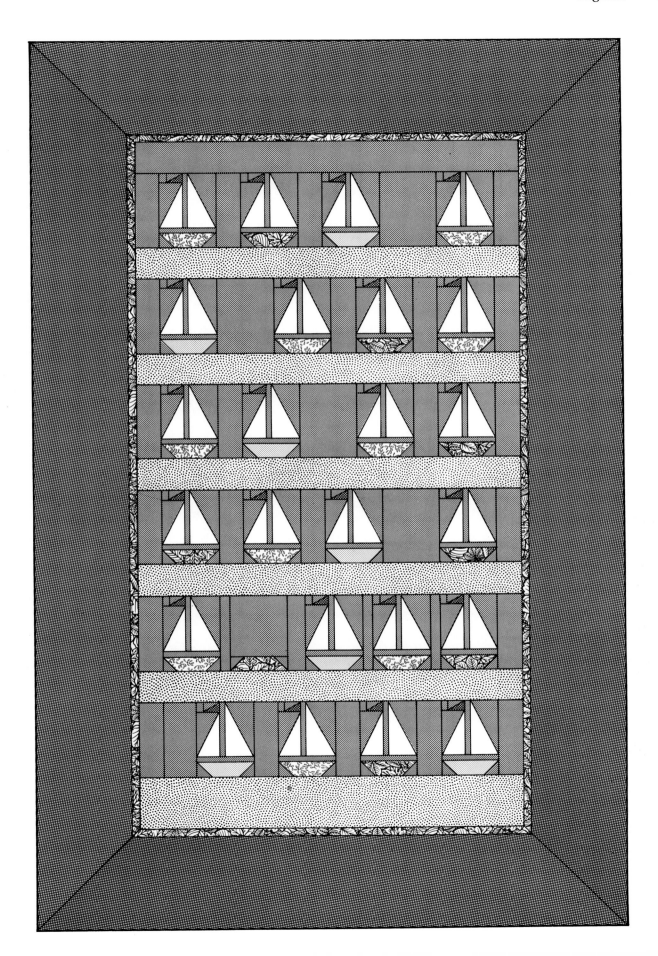

Pondering the Goose

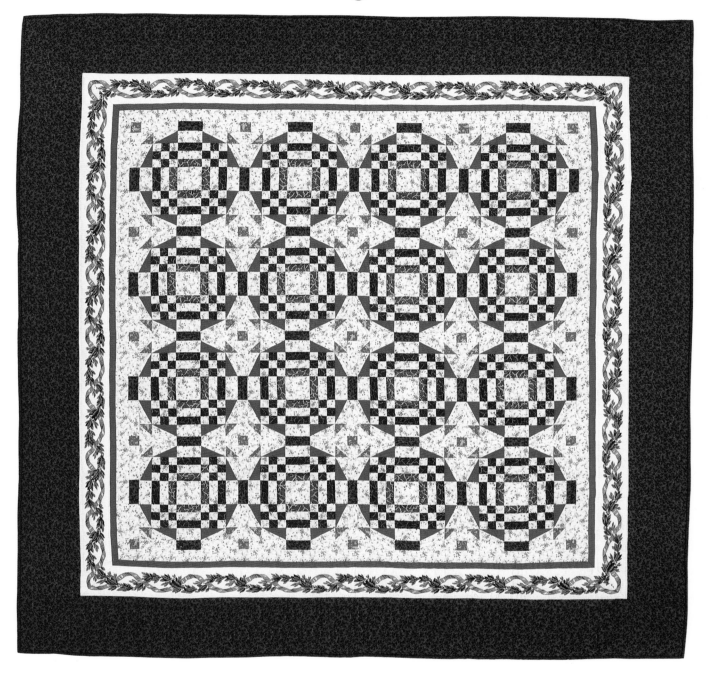

Pondering the Goose *by Mary Hickey, 1990, Seattle, Washington, 80½" x 80½". An unusual decorator fabric sets the color scheme for this Christmas quilt.*

Block size (finished): 12"
Pieced area of quilt: 54¼" x 54¼"
Quilt with borders: 80½" x 80½"

Materials (44"–45"wide fabric)

3 yds. fabric A (background)
¾ yd. fabric B (main)
1 yd. fabric C (Ninepatches and three-line squares)
⅝ yd. fabric D (bias squares and set squares)
¼ yd. fabric E (rectangular set pieces)
⅜ yd. inner border fabric
1¼ yds. middle border fabric
1⅞ yds. outer border fabric (fabric E)

Optional templates (for scissors cutting): 1, 2, 3, 11, 12, 13, 14, 15

Unit Instructions

BIAS RECTANGLES

 2" x 3½"

1. Cut: 2 pieces fabric A, 12" x 42"
   2 pieces fabric B, 12" x 42"
2. Following the instructions on pages 14–17, cut and sew 128 bias rectangles. You need 64 with fabric B on the right and 64 with fabric B on the left.

SQUARES AND RECTANGLES

1. Cut 5 strips fabric A, 3½" x 42".
2. Cut 2 of the strips into 3½" squares. You need 16. There will be some of the second strip left over.

3½" x 3½"

3. Cut 3 of the strips into 2" x 3½" rectangles. You need 64. You may need to use leftover fabric from step 2.

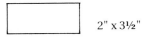 2" x 3½"

NINEPATCHES AND THREE-LINE SQUARES

1. Cut: 18 strips fabric A, 1½" x 42"
   21 strips fabric C, 1½" x 42"
2. Sew 8 of the fabric A strips and 16 of the fabric C strips into 8 units made up of C-A-C as illustrated.

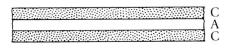
C
A
C

3. Cut 6 of these units into 3½" three-line squares. You need 64 three-line squares. You will have about 28" left over.

4. From the 28" left over in step 3 and from the two remaining units, cut 1½" x 3½" rectangles. You need 64 rectangles.

5. Sew 10 of the fabric A strips and 5 of the fabric C strips into 3 units made up of A-C-A as illustrated.

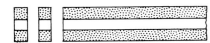
A
C
A

6. Cut across these units, creating 1½" rectangles. You need 128 rectangles.
7. Using the rectangles cut in steps 4 and 6, stitch 64 Ninepatches.

BIAS SQUARES

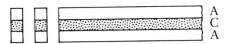 2" x 2"

1. Cut: 1 piece fabric A, 9" x 42"
   1 piece fabric D, 9" x 42"
2. Following the instructions on pages 17–18, cut and sew 64 bias squares. Cut the strips 2¼" wide. Cut 2" bias squares.

Assemble the blocks as illustrated.

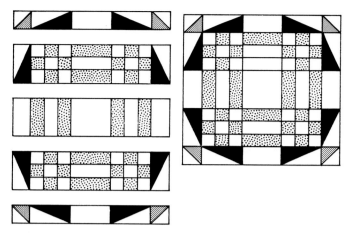

Sashing

1. Cut 10 strips fabric A, 1¾" x 42".
2. Cut the strips into rectangles, 1¾" x 5". You need 80 rectangles.

    ⬜ 1¾" x 5"

3. Cut 4 strips of fabric E, 1¾" x 42".
4. Cut the strips into rectangles, 1¾" x 3½". You need 40 rectangles.

    ⬛ 1¾" x 3½"

5. Cut 2 strips fabric D, 1¾" x 42".
6. Cut the strips into 1¾" squares. You need 25 squares.

    ▩ 1¾" x 1¾"

Assembling the Quilt Top

1. Sew the rectangles end to end as illustrated.

2. Stitch the sashing units between the blocks to create 4 rows of blocks. Be careful to match the corners as you sew.

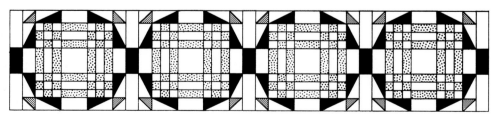

Sew a sashing unit on the ends of each row

3. Sew a sashing unit on the ends of each row.
4. Stitch the squares between the remaining sashing units to make 5 long sashing strips.

5. Sew the long sashing strips between the rows to make the quilt top.
6. Sew the 2 remaining long sashing strips to the top and bottom of the quilt top as shown on page 47.

Borders

1. Cut and sew 4 inner borders, 1¼" x 56¾".
2. Cut and sew 4 middle borders, 5" x 66¾".
3. Cut and sew 4 outer borders, 8" x 82¾".
4. Sew the borders to each other.
5. Stitch the borders to the quilt top, mitering the corners (see Mitering Corners, pages 76–77). Trim as necessary.

Finishing

1. Layer the quilt top with batting and backing.
2. Baste, quilt, and bind.

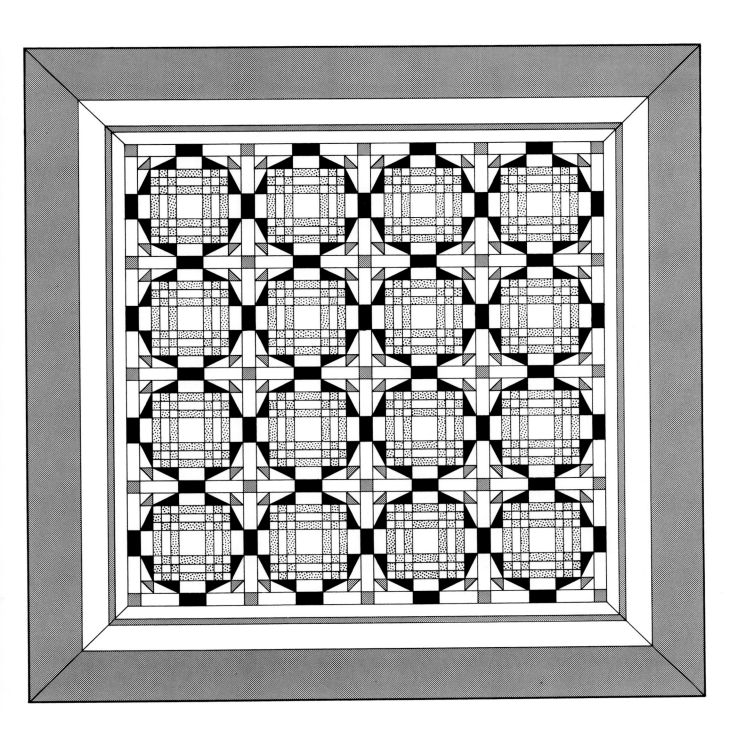

Stars All Around

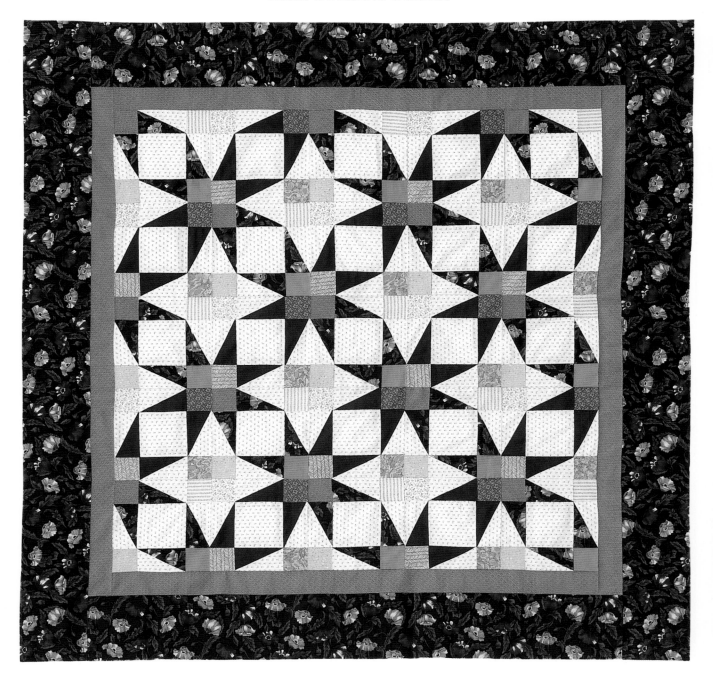

Stars All Around *by Suzanne Nelson, 1990, Seattle, Washington, 41½" x 41½". These simple blocks in two different fabric combinations blend to produce a dynamic pattern.*

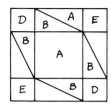 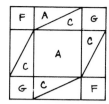

Block size (finished): 6"
Pieced area of quilt: 30" x 30"
Quilt with borders: 41½" x 41½"

To complete each block, you need four bias triangles, one large square, and four small ones. The design is composed of blocks made with two different fabric combinations. Half of the blocks are sewn with fabrics A, B, D, and E; the other half are sewn with fabrics A, C, F, and G. The instructions that follow are for twenty-five 6" blocks. Since these simple squares are easy to cut, you can decide later if you want to make more blocks.

Materials (44"–45" wide fabric)

1 yd. fabric A (background)
⅓ yd. fabric B (bias rectangles)
⅓ yd. fabric C (bias rectangles)
⅛ yd. each of 4 different fabrics: D, E, F, and G (corner squares)
¼ yd. inner border fabric
⅝ yd. outer border fabric

Optional templates (for scissors cutting): 1, 2, 14

Unit Instructions

BIAS RECTANGLES

2" x 3½"

1. Cut: 2 pieces fabric A, 12" x 42"
      1 piece fabric B, 12" x 42"
      1 piece fabric C, 12" x 42"
2. Following the instructions on pages 14–17, cut and sew 100 bias rectangles. You need 25 bias rectangles with fabric B on the right and 25 with fabric B on the left. You also need 25 with fabric C on the right and 25 with fabric C on the left:

      25   AB
      25   BA
      25   AC
      25   CA

SQUARES

1. Cut 2 strips fabric A, 3½" x 42".

2. Layer the strips and cut them into 3½" squares. You will get 24 from 2 strips, but you need 25. So, cut 1 more. If you know you want to make more blocks, cut 3 strips, layer them, and cut them all at once.

3½" x 3½"

3. Layer D, E, F, and G and cut 2 strips, each 2" x 42". Cut these strips into 2" squares. You need 25 each of the 4 different fabrics for a total of 100 squares.

2" x 2"

Assembling the Blocks

1. The blocks in this quilt are stitched directly to each other without sashing or set blocks. To make it easier to match all the points, designate blocks as either A or B and press to obtain opposing seams (see page 19).

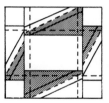 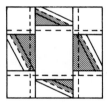

Block A
Press all seams
toward squares

Block B
Press all seams
toward triangles

2. Arrange several A blocks on your work surface so that you can chain piece them. I find it helpful to establish an order for each fabric and to arrange the blocks so that they are all pointing the same direction.
3. Stitch the A block pieces together in rows.

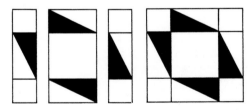

4. Press all seams toward the squares.
5. Sew the rows together to create the blocks.
6. Press the seams toward the outside of the block.
7. Arrange several B blocks on your work surface, following your color order and pointing them all in the same direction.

8. Sew the pieces together in rows.

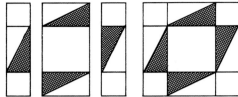

9. Press all seams toward the triangles.
10. Sew the rows together to make the blocks.
11. Press the seams toward the center of the block.

Assembling the Quilt Top

1. Sew the blocks together in rows, alternating the A and B blocks.
2. Press toward the A blocks.
3. Sew the rows together to make the quilt top.

Borders

1. Cut 4 strips inner border fabric, 2" x 34".
2. Cut 4 strips outer border fabric, 4½" x 42".
3. Sew the borders to the quilt top, mitering the corners (see Mitering Corners, pages 76–77).

Finishing

1. Layer the quilt top with batting and backing.
2. Baste, quilt, and bind.

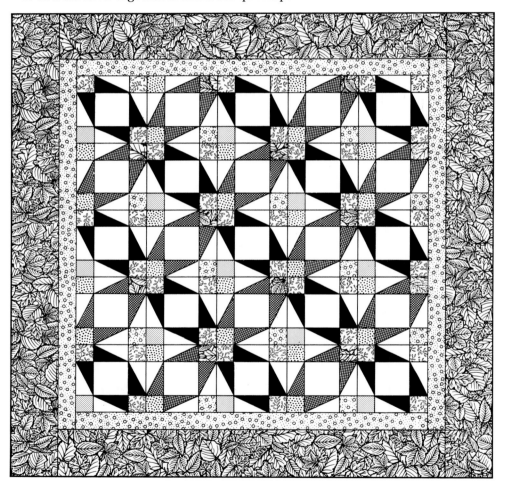

Star Waves

Gem Star (Star Waves) *by Judy Sogn, 1990, Seattle, Washington, 78" x 90". In this interesting block, the negative space (the background) is more dynamic than the pattern space. If the blocks are set together side by side, large circles are formed, and the quilt is reminiscent of the 1930s Bailey's Ninepatch. When the blocks are shifted, as in this quilt, a graceful zigzag is formed.*

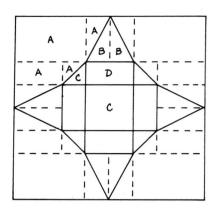

Block size (finished): 12"
Pieced area of quilt: 60" x 72"
Quilt with borders: 78" x 90"

Materials (44"–45" wide fabric)

4 yds. fabric A (background)
1½ yds. fabric B (main)
1¾ yds. fabric C (bias squares)
¾ yd. fabric D (accent)
¾ yd. inner border fabric
1½ yds. outer border fabric

Optional templates (for scissors cutting): 1, 2, 3, 14, 16

Unit Instructions

BIAS RECTANGLES

   2" x 3½"

1. Cut: 4 pieces fabric A, 12" x 42"
       4 pieces fabric B, 12" x 42"
2. Following the instructions on pages 14–17, cut and sew 240 bias rectangles. You need 120 with fabric B on the right and 120 with fabric B on the left.

RECTANGLES AND SQUARES
1. Cut 10 strips fabric A, 2" x 42".
2. Layer the strips and cut into 2" x 3½" rectangles. You need 120.

2" x 3½"

3. Cut 10 strips fabric A, 5" x 42".
4. Layer the strips and cut into 3½" x 5" rectangles. You need 120.

3½" x 5"

5. Cut 3 strips fabric C, 3½" x 42".
6. Layer the strips and cut into 3½" squares. You need 28. These are the center squares.

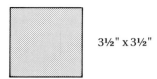   3½" x 3½"

7. From the pieces of the strips that remain, cut 4 rectangles that are 2" x 3½". These will be used in the half blocks.

    2" x 3½"

8. Cut 10 strips fabric D, 2" x 42".
9. Layer the strips and cut them into 2" x 3½" rectangles. You need 116.

    2" x 3½"

10. From the pieces of the strips that remain, cut 8 squares, 2" x 2". These will be used in the half blocks.

    2" x 2"

BIAS SQUARES

   2" x 2"

1. Cut: 2 pieces fabric A, 9" x 42"
       2 pieces fabric C, 9" x 42"
2. Following the instructions on pages 17–18, cut and sew 120 bias squares. Cut the strips 2¼" wide and cut 2" bias squares. You need 120 of them.

Assembling the Blocks

1. Sew 28 full blocks.

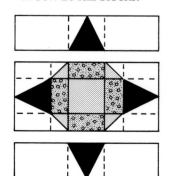
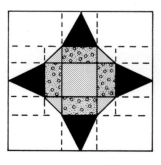

2. Sew 4 half blocks.

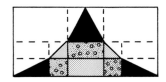

Assembling the Quilt Top

1. Stitch the blocks together in vertical rows.
2. Sew 3 rows of 6 blocks each, 2 rows of 5 blocks each, and 2 half blocks.
3. Sew the rows together to make the quilt top.

Borders

1. Cut and sew: 2 inner borders, 3" x 70"
                     2 inner borders, 3" x 82"
2. Cut and sew: 2 outer borders, 6" x 82"
                     2 outer borders, 6" x 94"
3. Stitch the borders to each other in pairs.
4. Sew the borders to the quilt top, mitering the corners (see Mitering Corners, pages 76–77). Trim as necessary.

Finishing

1. Layer the quilt with batting and backing.
2. Baste, quilt, and bind.

Rain Barrel

Rain Barrel *by Lyn Boland, 1990, Seattle, Washington, 52½" x 66". When the Rain Barrel blocks are placed side by side, a secondary pattern that is stronger than the block pattern forms. The use of soft colors and half blocks in the border enhances the secondary design and makes the block more versatile.*

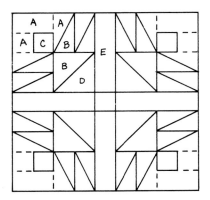

Block size (finished): 13½"
Center pieced area of quilt: 40½" x 54"
Quilt with pieced border: 52½" x 66"

The unusual border effect used in this quilt is achieved by making half blocks in a slightly darker color combination.

Materials (44"–45" wide fabric)

1⅝ yds. fabric A (background)
2 yds. fabric B (main and border)
¼ yd. fabric C (accent squares)
¾ yd. fabric D (bias squares and border)
½ yd. fabric E (long rectangles)
1¼ yds. border background (fabric D)
¾ yd. border bias rectangles (fabric B)

Optional templates (for scissors cutting): 1, 2, 3, 4, 18

Unit Instructions for Center Blocks

2" x 3½"

1. Cut: 3 pieces fabric A, 12" x 42"
   3 pieces fabric B, 12" x 42"
2. Following the instructions on pages 14–17, cut and sew 192 bias rectangles. You need 96 with fabric B on the right and 96 with fabric B on the left.

Rectangles and Squares

1. Cut 4 strips fabric A, 2" x 42".
2. Layer the strips and cut into 2" x 3½" rectangles. You need 48.

2" x 3½"

3. Cut: 4 strips fabric A, 2" x 42"
   4 strips fabric C, 2" x 42"
4. Sew the strips together in pairs and press toward the darker color.
5. Layer the sewn strips and cut across them to create 2" two-patch rectangles. You need 48 of them.

6. Cut 8 strips fabric E, 2" x 42".
7. Layer the strips and cut into rectangles, 2" x 6½".

2" x 6½"

8. Cut 1 strip fabric D, 2" x 42".
9. Cut the strip into 2" squares. You need 12 of them for the center of the blocks. If you prefer to vary the center squares, simply cut a variety of 2" squares.

2" x 2"

Bias Squares

3½" x 3½"

1. Cut: 2 pieces fabric B, 12" x 42"
   2 pieces fabric D, 12" x 42"
2. Following the instructions on pages 17–18, cut and sew 80 bias squares. Cut the strips 3¼" wide. Cut 3½" bias squares. Use 48 of the bias squares in the center blocks and 32 in the border half blocks.

Assembling the Center Blocks

1. The blocks in this quilt are stitched directly to each other without sashing or set blocks. To make it easier to match all points, designate blocks as either A or B and press to obtain opposing seams (see page 19).

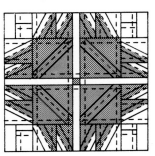

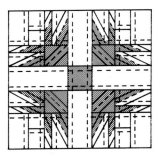

Block A
Press toward
lighter colors

Block B
Press toward
darker colors

2. Assemble the blocks as illustrated.

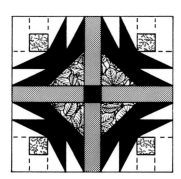

7. Cut 3 of the strips into rectangles, 2" x 6½". You need 14 rectangles.

2" x 6½"

8. Cut 3 of the strips into rectangles, 2" x 3½". You need 32 rectangles.

2" x 3½"

Assembling the Border Blocks

1. Designate half of the half blocks as A blocks and half as B blocks (see page 19).
2. Assemble the blocks as illustrated.
3. As you stitch together the units of the A blocks, press all seams toward the lighter color. As you sew the B blocks, press all seams toward the darker color.
4. Leave the center seams of 2 of the half blocks unsewn to create 4 quarter blocks for the outer corners.

Assembling the Quilt Top

1. Sew the blocks together into rows, alternating the A and B blocks.
2. Sew the border half blocks on the ends of the rows.
3. Stitch the remaining half blocks into 2 rows for the top and bottom borders.
4. Sew a quarter block on the end of each top and bottom border.
5. Stitch the rows together to make the quilt top as shown on page 57.

Finishing

1. Layer the quilt top with batting and backing.
2. Baste, quilt, and bind.

Unit Instructions for Border Blocks

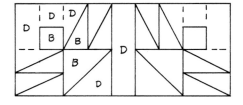

2" x 3½"

1. Cut: 2 pieces fabric D, 12" x 42"
   2 pieces fabric B, 12" x 42"
2. Following the instructions on pages 14–17, cut and sew 128 bias rectangles. You need 64 with fabric B on the right and 64 with fabric B on the left.
3. Cut: 3 strips fabric D, 2" x 42"
   3 strips fabric B, 2" x 42"
4. Sew the strips together in pairs.
5. Layer the sewn pairs of strips and cut across them to make two-patch rectangles. You need 32 two-patch rectangles.

6. Cut 6 strips fabric D, 2" x 42".

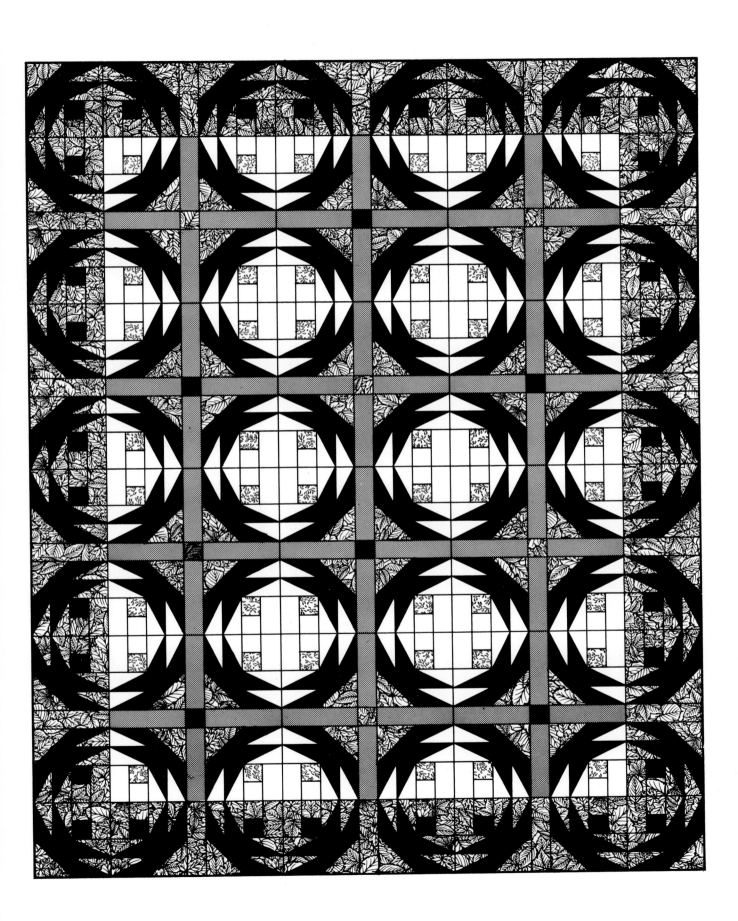

Drumbeat

Drumbeat *by Liz Thoman, 1990, Bellevue, Washington, 82" x 82". Fascinating patterns undulate across this quilt. The use of a decorative stripe in the corners of the center blocks emphasizes the circular forms that appear to weave from one block to another.*

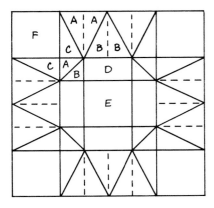

Block size (finished): 12"
Pieced area of quilt: 54" x 54"
Quilt with borders: 82" x 82"

Notice in the photograph how the quiltmaker cleverly solved the problem of not having quite enough border fabric for her quilt. She had a skirt made from the same fabric. Should she piece strips of the teal into the borders to "stretch" the border fabric or should she cut up her skirt? What a difficult decision! But she made a good choice.

Materials (44"–45" wide fabric)

5½ yds. fabric A (background)
2½ yds. fabric B (dark bias rectangles and bias squares)
1½ yds. fabric C (light bias rectangles)
¾ yd. fabric D (accent rectangles)
⅓ yd. fabric E (center squares)
¾ yd. fabric F (corner squares of blocks)
½ yd. inner border fabric
2 yds. outer border fabric

Optional templates (for scissors cutting): 1, 2, 13, 14

Unit Instructions

BIAS RECTANGLES

2" x 3½"

1. Cut: 3 pieces fabric A, 12" x 42"
   3 pieces fabric B, 12" x 42"
2. Following the instructions on pages 14–17, cut and sew 200 bias rectangles. You need 100 with fabric B on the right and 100 with fabric B on the left.

2" x 3½"

3. Cut: 3 pieces fabric A, 12" x 42"
   3 pieces fabric C, 12" x 42"
4. Following the instructions on pages 14–17, cut and sew 200 bias rectangles. You need 100 with fabric C on the right and 100 with fabric C on the left.

BIAS SQUARES

2" x 2"

1. Cut: 1 piece fabric A, 12" x 42"
   1 piece fabric B, 12" x 42"
2. Following the instructions on pages 17–18, cut and sew 100 bias squares. Cut the strips 2¼" wide. Cut 2" squares.

RECTANGLES

1. Cut 9 strips fabric D, 2" x 42".
2. Cut the strips into 2" x 3½" rectangles. You need 100 rectangles.

2" x 3½"

SQUARES

1. Cut 2 strips fabric E, 3½" x 42".
2. Cut the fabric E strips into 3½" squares. You need 25 but you will only get 24 from the 2 strips, so cut 1 more square. These are the center squares.

3½" x 3½"

3. Cut 3 strips fabric A, 3½" x 42.
4. Cut the fabric A strips into 3½" squares. You need 36 squares. These will be the corner squares for the blocks on the outside edges of the quilt top.

3½" x 3½"

5. Cut 6 strips of fabric F, 3½" x 42. Notice that this fabric is used only in the center blocks and in the inner corners of the blocks on the outside rows. In the quilt in the photograph, the quiltmaker has used a striped fabric and cut the squares on the bias. By varying the area from which she cut the stripes, she obtained an intricate-looking secondary pattern.
6. Cut the strips into 3½" squares. You need 64 squares.

3½" x 3½"

Assembling the Blocks

1. The blocks in this quilt are stitched directly to each other without sashing or set blocks. To make it easier to match all points, designate blocks as either A or B and press to obtain opposing seams (see page 19).

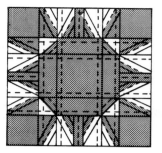

Block A
Press toward
outside of block

Block B
Press toward
center of block

2. As you designate the A and B blocks, you still have the problem of the corner squares made of fabric A and the corner squares made of fabric F. I suggest you make the 16 inner blocks, alternating them as A blocks and B blocks. Then, arrange the pieces of the outer blocks around the inner section of the quilt and with each block decide whether it should be an A or a B block. Then, sew and press accordingly.
3. Assemble the blocks as illustrated.

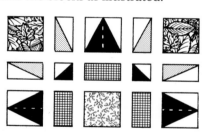

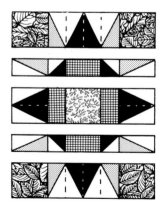

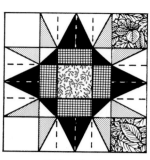

Center block   Side block

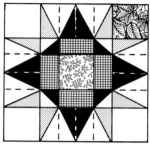

Corner block

Assembling the Quilt Top

1. Sew the blocks together into rows, alternating A and B blocks.
2. Stitch the rows together to make the quilt top as shown on page 61.

Borders

1. Cut and sew 4 strips inner border fabric, 1½" x 58".
2. Stitch the inner borders to the quilt. Trim borders as necessary.
3. Cut and sew 4 strips outer border fabric, 7" x 84".
4. Sew the borders to the quilt top.

Finishing

1. Layer the quilt top with batting and backing.
2. Baste, quilt, and bind.

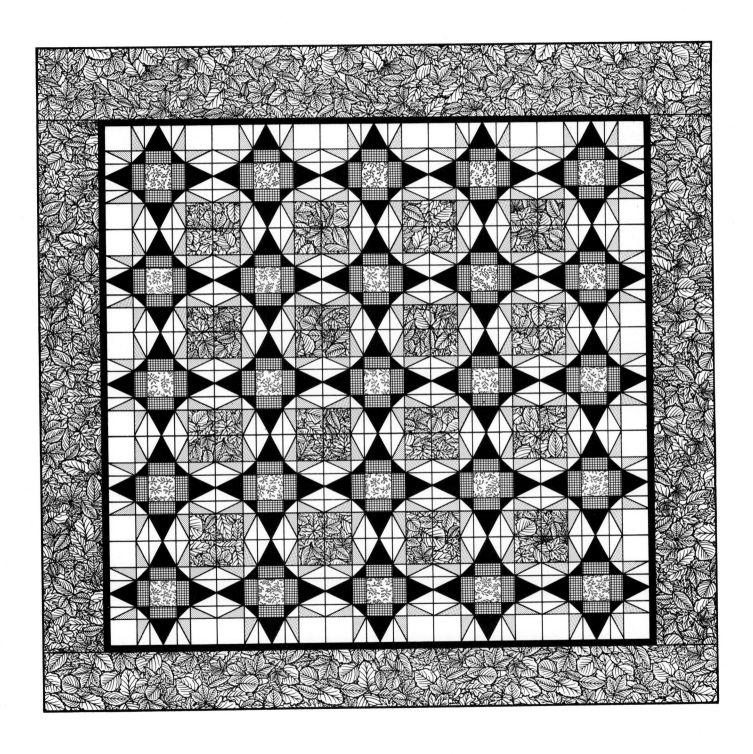

Wheat Flowers

Wheat Flowers *by Judy Pollard, 1990, Seattle, Washington, 38" x 43". Bias rectangles combined with squares create this innovative flower in an exotic bouquet.*

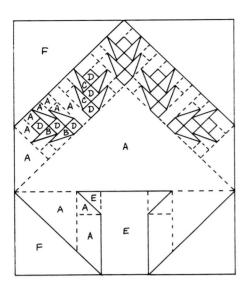

Center block size (finished): 25"
Pieced area of quilt: 27" x 33"
Quilt with borders: 38" x 43"

Materials: (44"–45" wide fabric)

1½ yds. fabric A (background)
¼ yd. fabric B (main flower)
¼ yd. fabric C (second flower)
⅛ yd. fabric D (flower center squares)
¼ yd. fabric E (vase)
½ yd. fabric F (set triangles)
½ yd. fabric G (stems and leaves)
⅛ yd. inner border fabric
¾ yd. outer border fabric (1¼ yds. if fabric has a directional design)

Optional templates: 1, 2, 3, 4, 18, 22, 23

Unit Instructions

BIAS RECTANGLES

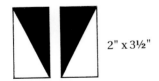

2" x 3½"

1. Cut: 1 piece fabric A, 9" x 21"
   1 piece fabric B, 9" x 21"
2. Following instructions on pages 14–17, cut and sew 12 bias rectangles. You need 6 bias rectangles with fabric B on the left and 6 with fabric B on the right.

2" x 3½"

3. Cut: 1 piece fabric A, 9" x 21"
   1 piece fabric C, 9" x 21"
4. Following instructions on pages 14–17, cut and sew 8 bias rectangles. You need 4 rectangles with fabric C on the right and 4 with fabric C on the left.

RECTANGLES AND SQUARES

1. Cut 2 strips fabric A, 2" x 42".
2. From 1 of these strips, cut 5 rectangles, 2" x 3½".

2" x 3½"

3. From the rest of this strip, cut 2 rectangles, 2" x 6½".

2" x 6½"

4. From the remaining strip, cut 2" squares. You need 15 squares.

2" x 2"

VASE

1. Cut 2 rectangles from fabric A, 3½" x 8½". These will be sewn along the side of the vase and then trimmed.
2. Cut 1 rectangle from fabric A, 6½" x 11½".
3. Use Template #4 on page 87 to cut 2 triangles from fabric A and 2 triangles from fabric E. Stitch these 4 triangles into 2 squares. These squares will form the lip of the vase.

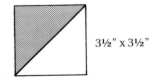

3½" x 3½"

4. Cut a 12¼" square from fabric A. Cut the square in half on the diagonal and in half again on the other diagonal. You should have 4 triangles with the straight grain on the long sides. Place 2 of them with the units that will be sewn together to create the vase section of the quilt.

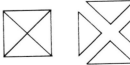

5. Layer the remaining 2 triangles cut in step 4 and cut ¾" off their long sides as illustrated. These triangles will be sewn together with the flower section.

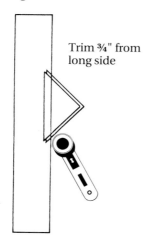

Trim ¾" from long side

6. Cut 1 triangle fabric A, making the short sides each 19½" (the long side should measure 27⅝") with the straight grain on the short sides.

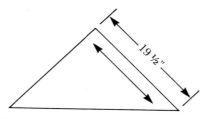

19 ½"

FLOWER CENTERS

1. Cut 1 strip fabric D, 2" x 42".
2. Cut the strip into 2" squares. You need 15. These will be the centers of the flowers.

2" x 2"

Assembling the Center Block

1. Assemble the flower section of the center block.

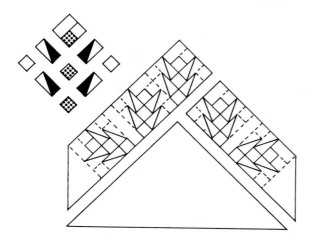

2. Assemble the vase section of the center block.

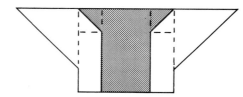

3. Sew the vase section to the flower section. Trim.
4. Cut 5 bias strips fabric G, 1¼" x 18", for stems. Templates for leaves are on page 87. Appliqué the stems and leaves to the center block (see pages 75–76 for further instructions on appliqué). After appliqué is complete, pluck open a few stitches of the seams and tuck in the ends of the stems. Then, stitch the seams closed again.

Set Triangles

1. Cut 1 square fabric F, 15" x 15". Cut the square in half on the diagonal. This will create 2 triangles to sew on the outside of the blossom section.

2. Sew the set triangles to the flower section of the center block.
3. Cut 1 square fabric F, 11⅞" x 11⅞". Cut the square in half on the diagonal. This will create 2 triangles to sew on the outside of the vase section of the block.
4. Sew the set triangles to the vase section. Trim off the ends of the background rectangles as illustrated.

Trim corners of rectangles

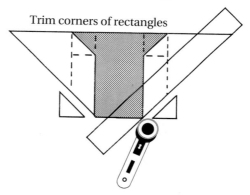

Borders

1. Cut: 2 strips inner border fabric, 1" x 33"
        2 strips inner border fabric, 1" x 29"
2. Stitch the inner borders to the quilt top. Sew the long sides first; trim the ends. Sew the top and bottom; trim the ends.
3. Cut: 2 strips outer border fabric, 5" x 34½"
        2 strips outer border fabric, 5" x 38"
4. Stitch the outer borders to the quilt top. Sew the long sides first; trim the ends. Sew the top and bottom; trim the ends.

Finishing

1. Layer the quilt top with batting and backing.
2. Baste, quilt, and bind.

Windsor Garden

Windsor Garden *by Mary Hickey, 1990, Seattle, Washington, 87" x 87". Cheerful reds, blues, and greens, along with a delicate decorator chintz, create a folk-art appearance in this spirited quilt.*

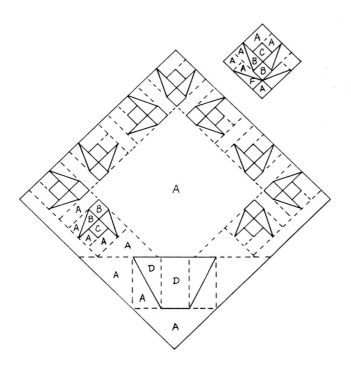

Center medallion size: 24" x 24"
Medallion with first pieced border: 48" x 48"
Border tulip block size (finished): 6"
Quilt with borders: 87" x 87"

Materials: (44"–45" wide fabric)

2½ yds. fabric A (background)
1¼ yds. fabric B (tulips)
¼ yd. fabric C (tulip center square)
2⅔ yds. fabric D (vase and borders)
2¾ yds. fabric E (chintz set squares and borders)
½ yd. fabric F (stems and leaves)

Optional templates (for scissors cutting): 1, 2, 3, 6, 17, 21, 24, 25

Unit Instructions

Bias Rectangles

2" x 3½"

1. Cut: 2 pieces fabric A, 12" x 42"
      2 pieces fabric B, 12" x 42"
   Since you need only 12 more bias rectangles than the 70 that you can efficiently cut from 1 set of fabrics, you could try using only 1 piece of each fabric. Cut 2½" strips from the large leftover triangles. Stitch these odd-shaped strips to the ends of your units to obtain the extra bias rectangles needed.

2. Following the instructions on pages 14–17, cut and sew 82 bias rectangles. You need 41 with fabric B on the right and 41 with fabric B on the left.

2" x 3½"

3. Cut: 3 pieces fabric A, 12" x 42"
      3 pieces fabric D, 12" x 42"
4. Following the instructions on pages 14–17, cut and sew 152 bias rectangles. You need 76 with fabric D on the right and 76 with fabric D on the left.

2" x 3½"

5. Cut: 1 piece fabric A, 12" x 42"
      1 piece fabric F, 12" x 42"
6. Following the instructions on pages 14–17, cut and sew 64 bias rectangles. You need 32 with fabric F on the right and 32 with fabric F on the left.

Center Medallion (flowers)

1. Cut 5 strips fabric A, 2" x 42".
2. From these strips, cut: 2 rectangles, 2" x 26"
                            2 rectangles, 2" x 11"

8 rectangles, 2" x 5"

9 rectangles, 2" x 3½"

9 squares, 2" x 2"

You will have some fabric left over. Save for the Tulip border blocks.

3. Cut 1 square fabric A, 14" x 14". This will be the large square on which the stems and leaves will be appliquéd.

4. Cut 1 square fabric A, 5¼" x 5¼". Cut this square in half on the diagonal.

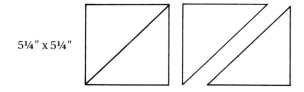

5¼" x 5¼"

5. Cut 1 strip fabric B, 2" x 42".
6. Cut the strip into 2" squares. You need 9 squares for the outside petals of the tulips in the center medallion. Save the rest of the strip for the outer portions of the quilt.

2" x 2"

7. Cut 1 strip fabric C, 2" x 42".
8. Cut the strip into 2" squares. You need 9 squares for the centers of the tulips in the center medallion. Save the rest of the strip for the outer portions of the quilt.

2" x 2"

This completes the cutting for the upper half of the center medallion. Stitch this much of the block together as illustrated.

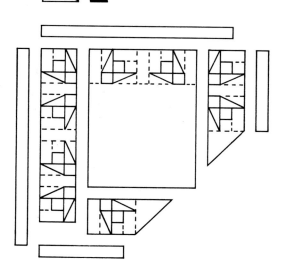

CENTER MEDALLION (VASE)

1. Cut and sew 2 bias rectangles from fabric A and 2 from fabric D. Cut the triangles 3½" x 6½".

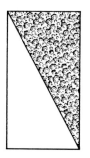
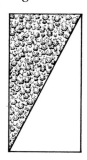

3½" x 6½"

2. Cut 1 rectangle fabric D, 3½" x 6½".

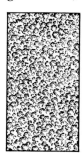

3½" x 6½"

3. Cut 1 square fabric A, 10" x 10". Cut the square in half on the diagonal and then in half again, creating 4 triangles. You only need 3 of them so 1 can go in your scrap bag.

This completes the cutting for the bottom half of the center medallion. Stitch together as illustrated.

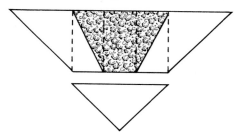

Assembling the Center Medallion

1. Stitch the top of the medallion to the bottom. Trim off the 3 small triangles on the top half that overlap the bottom half.

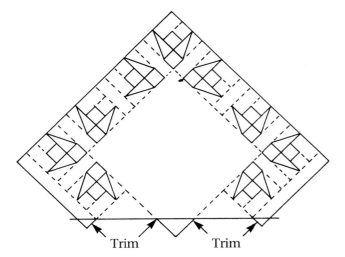

Trim   Trim

2. Cut 4 bias strips fabric F, 1" x 20", for stems. Cut 1 of the strips into shorter pieces for "branching" stems. Templates for leaves are on page 86. Appliqué the stems and leaves to the center medallion (see Appliqué, pages 75–76). After the appliqué is complete, pluck open a few stitches of the seams and tuck in the stems and leaves. Then, stitch the seams closed again.

First Border

1. Cut 4 strips fabric D, 2½" x 31".
2. Sew the borders to the quilt, mitering the corners (see Mitering Corners, pages 76–77).

Set Squares

1. Cut 2 squares fabric E, 22" x 22".
2. Cut the squares in half on the diagonal, creating 4 half-square triangles.

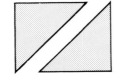

3. Stitch the triangles to the center medallion.
4. If necessary, trim the center medallion to a perfect square.

Inner Pieced Border

1. Stitch 4 border strips, each made up of 14 A-D bias rectangles from steps 3 and 4 under Bias Rectangles.

2. Sew 2 of the border strips to the sides of the center medallion.
3. Cut 4 squares fabric D, 2" x 2".
4. Stitch the squares to the ends of the 2 remaining border strips.

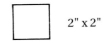

Stitch a square to each end

5. Sew the borders to the center medallion.
6. Cut: 2 strips fabric D, 2" x 42½"
   2 strips fabric D, 2" x 45½"
7. Sew the shorter strips to the sides of the center medallion and the longer ones to the top and bottom.
8. Cut: 2 strips fabric E, 4" x 48½"
   2 strips fabric E, 4" x 52½"
9. Sew the shorter strips to the sides of the medallion and the longer ones to the top and bottom. Trim as necessary.

Tulip Border Blocks

1. Cut 9 strips fabric A, 2" x 42".
2. Cut 6 of the strips into 2" squares. You need 128 squares. Use some of the squares left over from step 2, Center Medallion (flowers), page 67.

2" x 2"

3. Cut 3 of the strips into rectangles, 2" x 3½". You need 32 rectangles.

2" x 3½"

4. Cut: 1 strip fabric B, 2" x 42"
   1 strip fabric C, 2" x 42"
5. Layer the strips and cut them into 2" squares. Use the squares left over from step 6, Center Medallion (flowers), page 68. You need 32 squares of each fabric.

2" x 2"

6. Assemble 32 tulip blocks as illustrated.

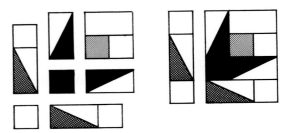

7. Cut 6 strips fabric A, 2" x 42".

8. Cut the strips into 2" x 6½" rectangles. You need 32 rectangles.

2" x 6½"

Finishing

1. Layer the quilt top with batting and backing.
2. Baste, quilt, and bind.

9. Sew 2 rows of 9 tulip blocks each, separating them with 2" x 6½" rectangles.

10. Sew 2 rows of 7 tulip blocks each, separating them with a 2" x 6½" rectangle. Stitch rectangles on both ends of these 2 rows.

11. Stitch the tulip rows to the quilt top. Sew the short rows to the sides first and then the longer rows to the top and bottom.

Outer Pieced Border

1. Cut 4 strips fabric A, 1½" x 70".
2. Sew 2 of the strips to the sides of the quilt; trim the ends. Sew the other 2 strips to the top and bottom; trim the ends.
3. Cut 4 strips fabric D, 2½" x 73".
4. Sew 2 of the strips to the sides of the quilt; trim the ends. Sew the other 2 strips to the top and bottom; trim the ends.
5. Stitch 4 borders, each made up of 24 bias rectangles.
6. Sew 2 of the borders to the sides of the quilt.
7. Cut 4 squares fabric D, 2½" x 2½".
8. Stitch the squares to the ends of the 2 remaining border strips.
9. Sew the borders to the quilt top.

Outer Borders

1. Cut: 2 strips fabric E, 4½" x 76"
   2 strips fabric E, 4½" x 83"
2. Sew the shorter strips to the sides of the quilt; trim the ends.
3. Sew the longer strips to the top and bottom; trim.
4. Cut: 2 strips fabric D, 2½" x 85"
   2 strips fabric D, 2½" x 88"
5. Sew the shorter strips to the sides of the quilt; trim the ends.
6. Sew the longer strips to the top and bottom; trim.

Meadowlark

Meadowlark *by Mary Hickey, 1990, Seattle, Washington, 81" x 81". Delicate pastels in combination with strong reds and navies create several secondary patterns in this radiant quilt.*

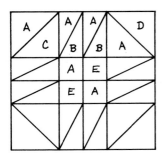

Block size (finished): 9"
Pieced area of quilt: 54" x 54"
Quilt with borders: 81" x 81"

Materials

(44"–45" wide fabric)
4⅓ yds. fabric A (background)
2 yds. fabric B (main)
¾ yd. fabric C (bias squares)
1 yd. fabric D (bias squares)
¼ yd. fabric E (Four Patches)
½ yd. inner border fabric
2½ yds. outer border fabric

Optional templates (for scissors cutting): 1, 2, 4

Unit Instructions

BIAS RECTANGLES

2" x 3½"

1. Cut: 5 pieces fabric A, 12" x 42"
     2 pieces fabric B, 12" x 42"
2. Following the instructions on pages 14–17, cut and sew 288 bias rectangles, 144 with fabric B on the right and 144 with fabric B on the left.

BIAS SQUARES

3½" x 3½"

1. Cut: 1 piece fabric A, 12" x 42"
     1 piece fabric C, 12" x 42"
2. Following the instructions on pages 17–18, cut and sew 72 bias squares. Cut the strips 3¼" wide. Cut 3½" bias squares.

3½" x 3½"

3. Cut: 1 piece fabric A, 12" x 42"
     1 piece fabric D, 12" x 42"
4. Following the instructions on pages 17–18, cut and sew 72 bias squares. Cut the strips 3¼" wide and cut 3½" bias squares.

FOUR PATCHES

1. Cut: 4 strips fabric A, 2" x 42"
     4 strips fabric E, 2" x 42"
2. Stitch the fabric A and fabric E strips together in pairs. Press toward the darker color.
3. Layer the sewn pairs of strips right sides together with opposite fabrics facing each other.

4. Cut across the sewn strips to create 2" x 3½" rectangles. You need 72 rectangles.

5. Stitch the rectangles together in pairs to create 36 Four Patches.

Assembling the Blocks

1. The blocks in this quilt are stitched directly to each other without sashing or set blocks. To make it easier to match all points, designate blocks as either A or B and press to obtain opposing seams (see page 19).

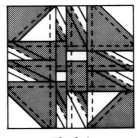
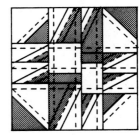

Block A
Press toward lighter colors

Block B
Press toward darker colors

2. Assemble the blocks as illustrated.

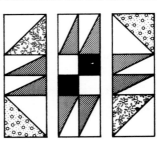
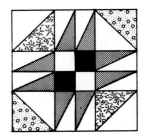

3. As you stitch together the units of the A blocks, press all seams toward the lighter color. As you sew the B blocks, press all seams toward the darker color.

Assembling the Quilt Top

1. Sew the blocks together in rows, alternating the A and B blocks.
2. Stitch the rows together to make the quilt top.

Borders

1. Cut and sew: 4 border strips fabric A, 2" x 60"
   4 border strips fabric B, 1½" x 65"
   4 border strips fabric D, 10" x 87"
2. Stitch the borders to each other.
3. Sew the borders to the quilt top, mitering the corners (see Mitering Corners, pages 76–77).

Finishing

1. Layer the quilt top with batting and backing.
2. Baste, quilt, and bind.

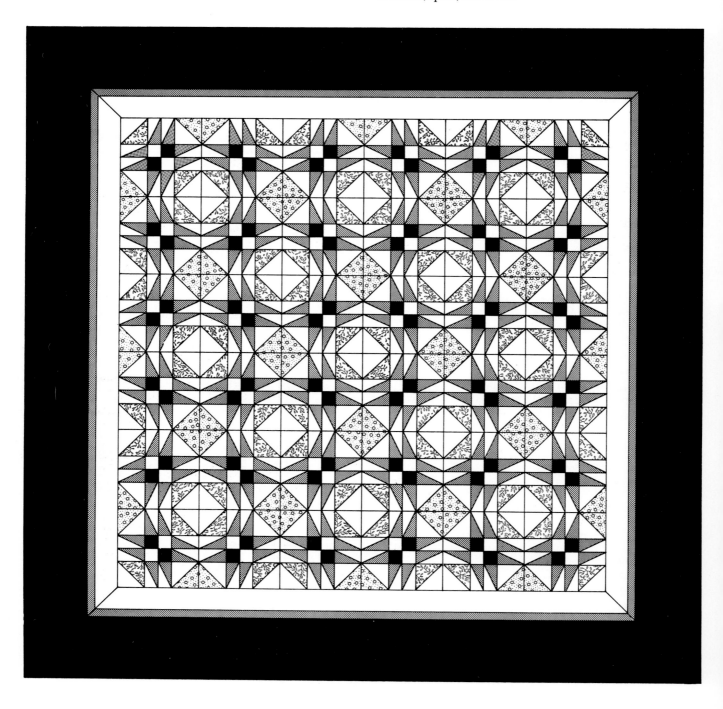

Glossary of Techniques

Appliqué

Appliqué, the securing of fabric shapes to a background, gives the quiltmaker a wide range of possibilities. When a quiltmaker appliqués, she first has to turn under a hem on the edges of each shape. These shapes are then sewn to the background with small, invisible stitches called blind stitches. Much of the charm of an appliqué pattern depends on the smoothness of the curves of the separate pieces.

Position the appliqué shapes by following the illustration in the quilt plan. A number sequence indicates the order of placement. Pin the shapes to the blocks and then machine baste them into position. Machine basting the shapes in position will anchor the pieces exactly where you want them and avoid the problem of pins poking your fingers and tangling the appliqué thread.

PAPER-PATCH APPLIQUÉ

In paper-patch appliqué, a stiff paper forms a base around which the fabric is shaped.

1. Trace each appliqué shape on stiff paper. (The subscription cards that come in magazines are the perfect weight.)

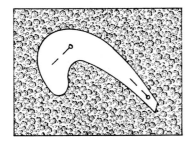

2. Cut out a paper template for each shape in the appliqué design. Appliqué templates are cut without seam allowances.
3. Pin each template to the wrong side of your appliqué fabric.

4. Cut out the fabric in the template shape, adding ¼" seam allowance.

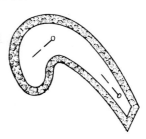

5. With your fingers, fold the seam allowance over the edge of the paper and baste it to the paper.
   a. Start with deep cleavages and inside curves. Clip these areas close to the paper to allow the fabric to stretch over the template.

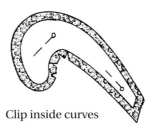

   Clip inside curves

   b. On outside curves, take small running stitches in the fabric only. This will allow you to ease the fullness over the template.

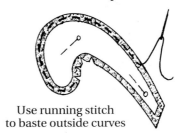

   Use running stitch
   to baste outside curves

   c. Points require some encouragement to lie flat and come to a sharp point. First, fold the tip over the paper; then, hold it in place while you fold the right side across the tip. Use a small, sharp scissors to cut away the extra fabric. Next, fold the left seam across the right one and trim it. Take two tiny basting stitches through the fabric folds and the paper to hold everything in place.

6. When all seam allowances have been basted onto the templates, press them with a warm iron.
7. Machine baste the shapes in position on the quilt block.
8. Use a blind stitch to appliqué the pieces to the quilt block (see illustration). Complete the appliqué; then, remove the basting stitches.

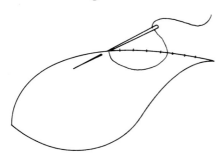

9. Working from the back of the quilt block, carefully snip the background fabric behind each shape and remove the paper.

BIAS-BAR STEMS

One of the most satisfying techniques for creating smooth, graceful stems uses metal or plastic bias bars. Bias or Celtic bars are sold in most quilt shops. The stems in this book can be made with either a ¼" or a ⅜" bar.

1. Cut bias strips the length specified in the quilt plan.

2. Fold the bias strip in half, wrong sides together; press.
3. Stitch ⅛" from the raw edge, creating a tube.

4. Insert the bias bar into the tube and twist the bar to bring the seam to the center of one of the bar's flat sides.

Twist bar to bring seam to center

5. Press the seam flat with a warm iron.

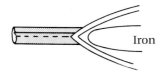

Iron

6. Remove the bar. (The bar will be hot, so be careful not to burn your fingers.)
7. The raw edge is now pressed out of sight on the underside of the tubing, and there are two evenly folded edges to appliqué.

8. Pin the stems into position. You are now ready to appliqué. If you find it a nuisance to stitch with the pins in the way, machine baste the stems in place.

9. After you have completed the appliqué, remove the pins or basting stitches. Pluck open a few stitches of the seams of the quilt block and tuck in the raw ends of the stems.

Borders

Fine works of art are greatly enhanced by careful framing. Thoughtfully planned and sewn borders function as frames for quilt designs. Each quilt plan in this book provides directions for one type of border treatment. Take some time to study the border treatments of the quilts pictured in the Gallery of Quilts and in the quilt plans. If you prefer a different treatment for your quilt than the one pictured, simply find the border design that you prefer in a different quilt plan and change the measurements to fit your quilt.

You will find a variety of border designs in *Angle Antics*. Take some time to study the elements of the border designs. Multiple strips of fabric are sewn together in Meadowlark (page 72) and a striped decorator fabric enhances Pondering the Goose (page 44). Jazzy stripes run perpendicular to the edges of the Regatta quilt (page 40). The sawtooth borders made of bias rectangles in Windsor Garden (page 66) add great elegance. Notice the wonderful jungle border on Drumbeat (page 54), with its "coping" strips to compensate for a lack of fabric.

However you compose your border, you will need to decide whether to sew the corners with blunt seams or mitered seams. For blunt-sewn corners, first sew the borders to the long sides of the quilt and then to the shorter sides.

Mitered corners are not difficult to make and are worth the added effort in many designs. The fabric requirements in the quilt plans include border requirements and allow a few extra inches for shrinkage. It is wise to cut border strips about 4"–6" longer than the length of the quilt. After the borders are sewn to the quilt top, they can be trimmed.

MITERING CORNERS

1. Measure your quilt and calculate the finished outside dimensions of the top. The quilt plans in this book have done this step. The measurements given include an extra 2"–4" to allow for variances in your quilt. This extra fabric should be trimmed after you have sewn the miter.
2. If you are using multiple borders, center the strips on each other and sew them together, creating striped fabric that can be treated as one unit.
3. Center the strips of border fabric on the sides of the quilt top.

4. Start stitching the borders to the quilt top ¼" from one end of the quilt and stop ¼" from the other end. Stitch the borders to all four sides of the quilt, leaving the first and last ¼" unsewn.
5. Arrange the quilt with one corner right side up on the ironing board.
6. Fold one border into a 45° angle with the other border. Work with the stripes so that they meet. Pin the fold, arranging the pins with all the heads facing the center of the quilt; press.

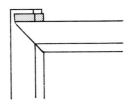

7. Use 1" masking tape to tape the mitered angle in place. Start at the outer edge of the quilt and carefully center the tape over the mitered fold as you remove the pins.

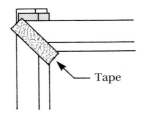
Tape

8. Turn the quilt over and draw a light pencil line on the crease created by pressing in step 6.
9. Stitch on the pencil line and remove the tape.
10. Trim away the excess fabric.
11. Repeat steps 5–10 on the remaining corners.

Marking

Carefully press the quilt top and trace the quilting designs on it. Use a sharp pencil and mark lightly. If you prefer to use a water-soluble pen, test for removability on a scrap before marking the quilt. Chalk dispensers and white pencils are available to mark dark fabrics. The quilt top may be marked for straight-line quilting with ½" masking tape after the quilt is basted.

Backing

Make a quilt backing that is 2" larger than your quilt top. Trim selvages to avoid puckers and press seams open. Spread the backing, wrong side up, over a clean, flat surface. Use masking tape to anchor the quilt to the surface without stretching it.

Batting

Batting is the filler between the backing and the top of the quilt. A lightweight cotton-polyester (80%-20%) batting works well. Battings of 100% cotton are also ex-

cellent but must be closely quilted to prevent shifting during laundering. Less quilting is needed with a 100% polyester bonded batting. However, some polyester may creep through the fabric and create tiny "beards" on the surface of the quilt. This problem is particularly noticeable on dark fabrics.

Basting

Spread the quilt batting over the backing, making sure it covers the entire backing and is smooth. Place the pressed and marked top over the batting. Center the quilt right side up over the batting. Align the borders and straight lines with the edges of the backing and pin baste carefully.

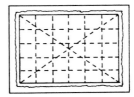

Baste the three layers together, using a long needle and light-colored quilting thread. If you thread your needle without cutting the thread off the spool, you will be able to baste at least one long row without rethreading your needle. Starting at the center of the quilt, use large stitches to baste an X on the quilt from corner to corner. Continue basting, creating a grid of parallel lines 8"–10" apart. Complete the basting with a line of stitches around the outside edges.

Quilting

Quilting is simply a short running stitch with a single thread that goes through all three layers of the quilt. Quilt on a frame, on a hoop, on a table top, or on your lap. Use quilting thread; it is thicker and less likely to tangle. A small (#10 or #12) needle will enable you to take small stitches. Cut the thread 20" long and tie a small knot. Starting about 1" from where you want the quilting to begin, insert the needle through the top and batting only. Gently tug on the knot until it pops through the quilt top and is caught in the batting. Take small, even, straight stitches through all layers.

To make small stitches, push the needle with a thimble on your middle finger. Insert the needle and push it straight down. Then, rock the needle up and down through all layers, "loading" three or four stitches onto the needle. Pull the needle through, aiming toward yourself as you work. Place your other hand under the quilt and use your thumbnail to make sure the needle has penetrated all three layers with each stitch.

To end a line of quilting, make a single knot close to the quilt top and then take a 1" stitch through the top and batting only. Clip the thread at the surface of the quilt. When all quilting is completed, remove the basting (except for the stitches around the edges).

Binding

Trim the batting and backing even with the quilt top. Cut 2" bias strips from the binding fabric. Seam the bias strips end to end to make a strip that is long enough to go all the way around the quilt plus about 6". Press a ½" hem on one long edge of the binding.

Starting just to the right of the center on one side and with the front of the quilt facing you, place the raw, unpressed edge of the binding on the edge of the quilt. Sew the binding to the quilt front using ¼" seams. Do not pin the binding to the quilt, but smooth it in place about 3" at a time without stretching it.

Stop your stitching ¼" from the end of the quilt and backtack.

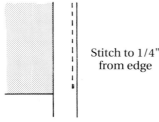

Stitch to 1/4"
from edge

Remove the quilt from the sewing machine. Push a pin from the back of the quilt up through your stitching line and ¼" from the end of the quilt. Fold the binding, creating a 45° angle. The binding should form a straight line out from the side that will be sewn next.

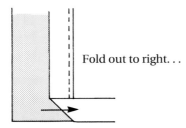

Fold out to right. . .

Hold the fold down with your finger and fold the rest of the binding back over itself to the edge that will be sewn next.

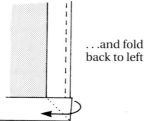

. . .and fold
back to left

Push the pin up through the very edge of the fold; start stitching at the point where the pin comes up through the binding (¼" from the corner).

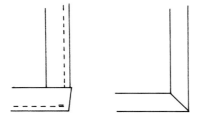

Continue around all four sides and corners of your quilt. When the binding is all stitched, place your finger under one of the corners and push the fold toward the point. Fold the fabric around to the back of the quilt and fold a miter on the back of the corner. Complete all four corners this way. Whipstitch the binding by hand onto the back of the quilt.

Labeling

Labeling your quilt is a nice finishing touch. You can embroider or cross-stitch your name, city, and the date on the back of your quilt. If you have too much information to stitch, you can letter a label with a permanent pen on muslin or even type the information on muslin and stitch it to the back.

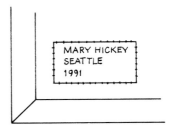

MARY HICKEY
SEATTLE
1991

Templates

Master Templates

This section provides templates for quilters who prefer a more traditional approach to quiltmaking. A number has been assigned to each template. The template numbers necessary for each quilt are listed with each quilt plan. The inner dotted line is the sewing line; the solid outer line is the cutting line and includes ¼" seam allowance.

BiRangle™ Templates

The BiRangle templates provided in this book will enable you to use the bias rectangle method, even if you are unable to obtain a BiRangle™. Trace the desired size, glue it to heavy cardboard or plastic, and cut out the rectangle. If you cannot see through the template, make sure that the ends of the diagonal lines are exactly on the seam lines of your strips.

Appliqué Templates

The appliqué templates provided in this book do not include seam allowances. Trace the appliqué templates onto heavy bond paper. Cut out the shapes and pin them to the wrong side of your fabric. Cut the shapes from your fabric, adding the seam allowances as you cut.

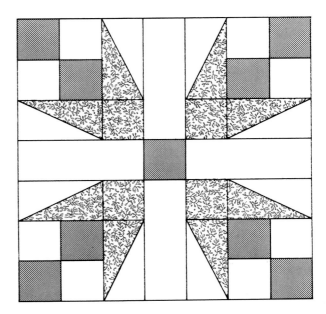

Master Templates

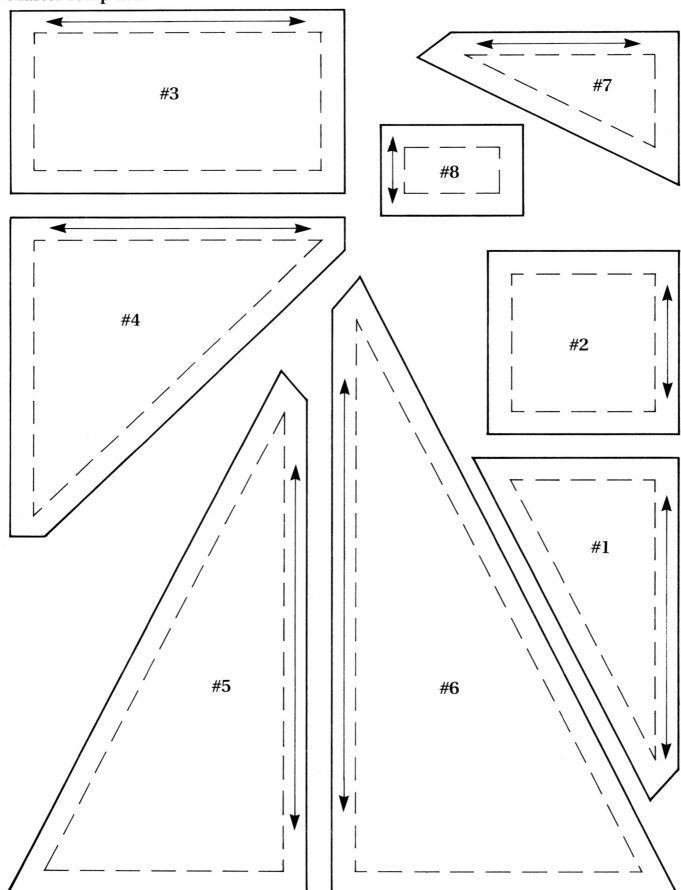

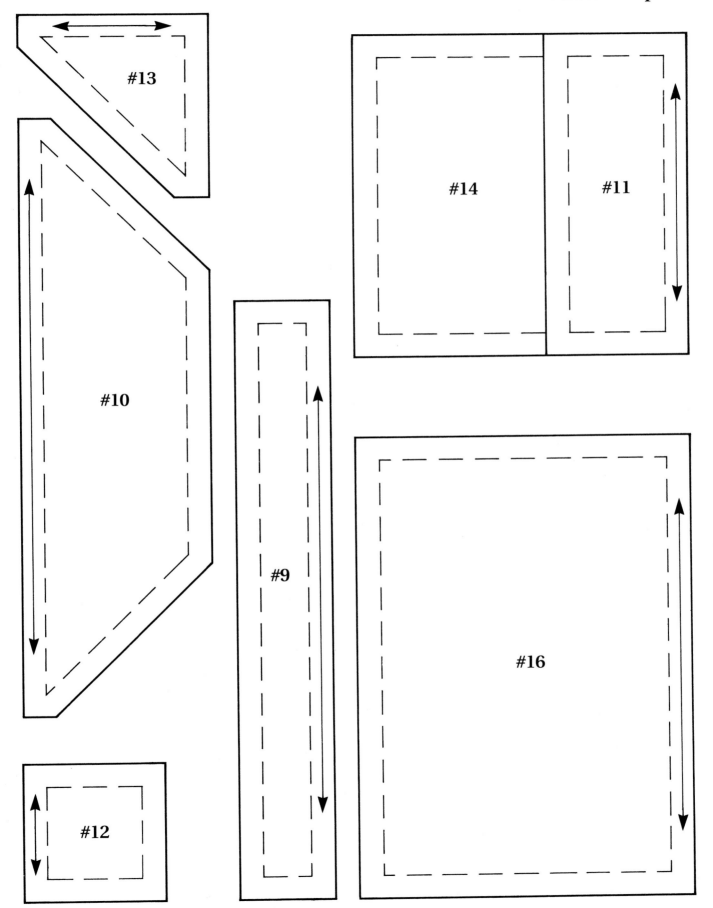

82

Master Templates

#17

Place on fold

#19

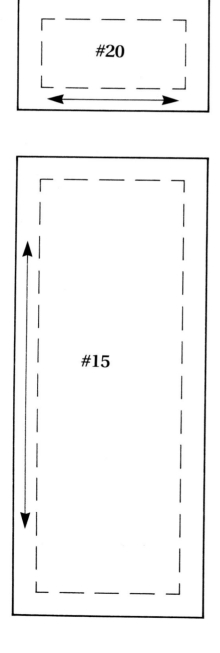

#20

#15

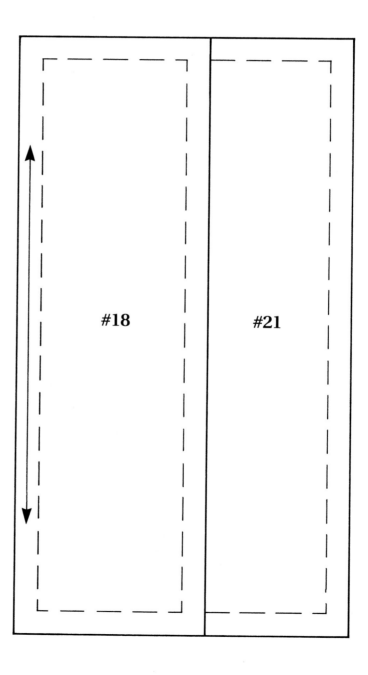

#18

#21

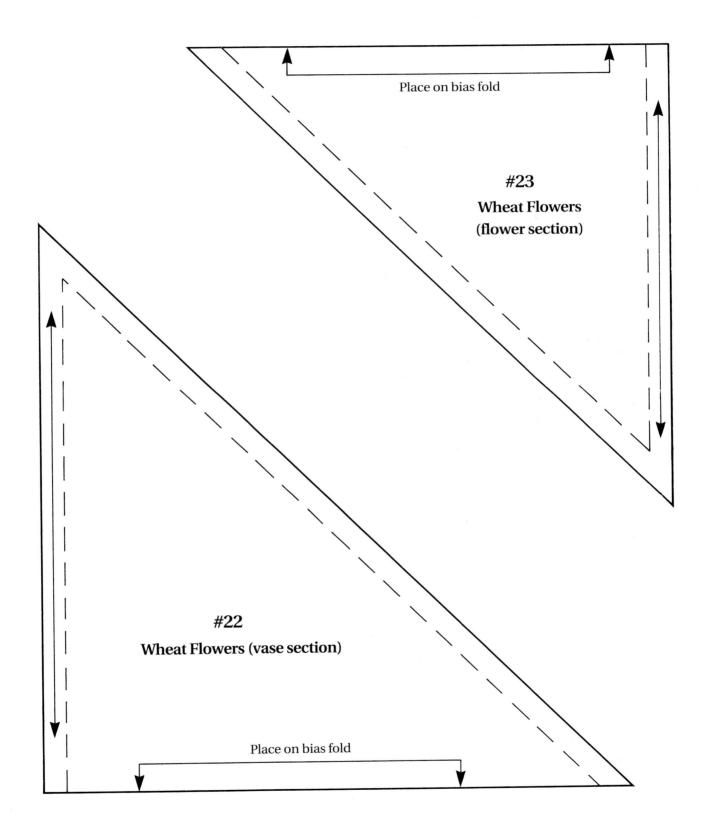

Place on bias fold

#23
Wheat Flowers
(flower section)

#22
Wheat Flowers (vase section)

Place on bias fold

Master Templates

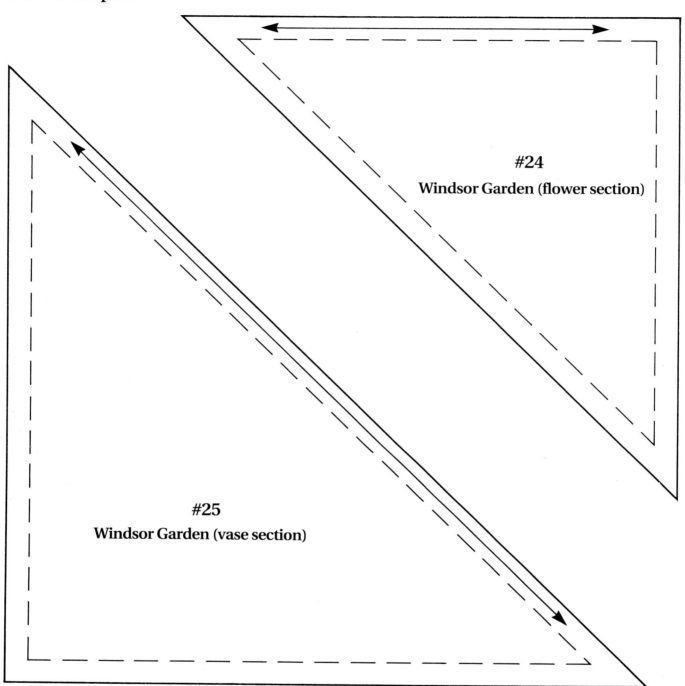

#24
Windsor Garden (flower section)

#25
Windsor Garden (vase section)

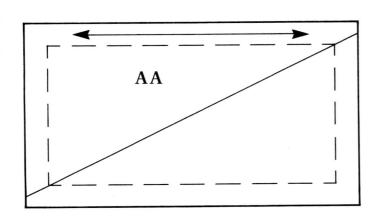

AA

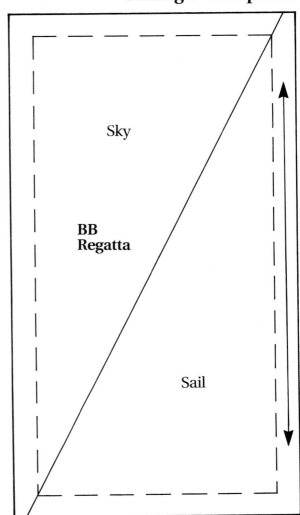

Sky

**BB
Regatta**

Sail

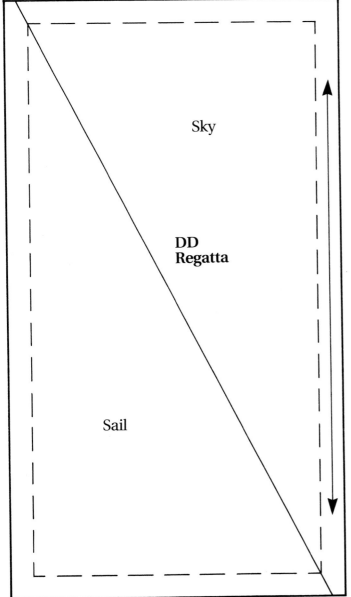

Sky

**DD
Regatta**

Sail

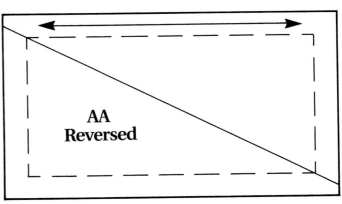

**AA
Reversed**

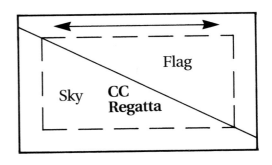

Flag

Sky **CC
Regatta**

Appliqué Templates

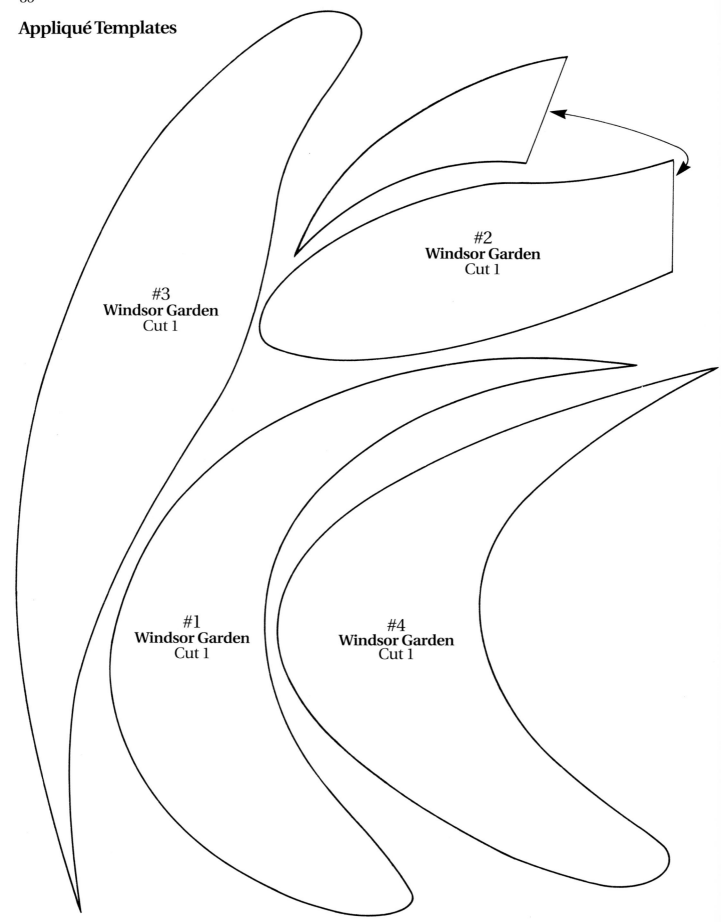

#3
Windsor Garden
Cut 1

#2
Windsor Garden
Cut 1

#1
Windsor Garden
Cut 1

#4
Windsor Garden
Cut 1

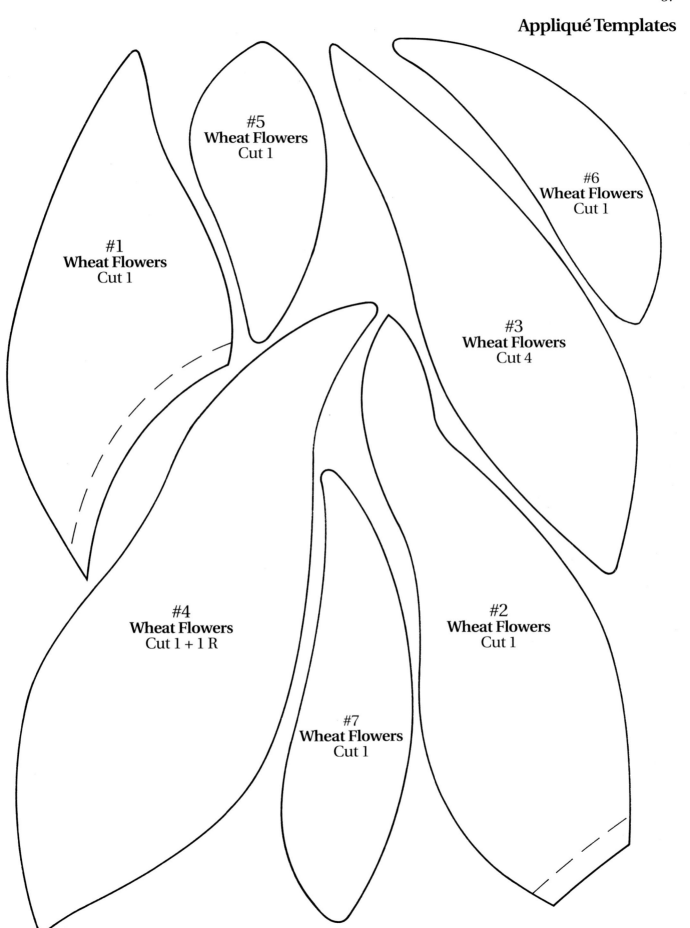

Appliqué Templates

#5
Wheat Flowers
Cut 1

#6
Wheat Flowers
Cut 1

#1
Wheat Flowers
Cut 1

#3
Wheat Flowers
Cut 4

#4
Wheat Flowers
Cut 1 + 1 R

#2
Wheat Flowers
Cut 1

#7
Wheat Flowers
Cut 1

That Patchwork Place Publications

Tools
6" Bias Square®
8" Bias Square®
Metric Bias Square®
BiRangle™
Pineapple Rule
Rotary Mate™
Rotary Rule™

For more information, send $2 for a color catalog to
That Patchwork Place, Inc., P.O. Box 118, Bothell, WA
98041-0118. Many titles should be available at your local
quilt shop.